HISTORY OF
SCOTLAND

HMP

HISTORY OF
SCOTLAND

CLIFF HANLEY

GALLERY BOOKS
An imprint of W.H. Smith Publishers Inc.
112 Madison Avenue
New York, New York 10016

A Bison Book

Published by Gallery Books
A Division of
W H Smith Publishers Inc.
112 Madison Avenue
New York, New York 10016

Produced by
Bison Books Corp.
17 Sherwood Place
Greenwich, CT 06830

ISBN 0-8317-4215-1

Printed in Belgium

1 2 3 4 5 6 7 8 9 10

Page 1: The religious reformer Andrew Melville
preaching to James VI in 1584.
Page 2-3: *Culloden* by David Morier, painted in 1746.
This page: Building the *Queen Elizabeth* at John
Brown's on the Clyde in 1938.

Contents

1 The Birth of a Nation

HUMAN BEINGS have lived in Scotland since the fourth millenium BC, at least. Where they came from it is impossible to tell; and why they came is obscure, because the climate was cold and wet and the landscape was forbidding. They huddled in caves or any other natural shelter they could find, made crude weapons and tools of stone.

Their staple diet was shellfish, but they hunted seals and fish, the deer and the boar, and covered themselves in animal skins. They knew nothing of farming. It is easy to forget that the modern landscape of Britain, with great areas of lush agricultural land, is man-made. Even a few centuries ago the fertile plains of Ayrshire were hard and unyielding.

Their skills developed over centuries, they made simple shelters, they found somehow – probably from invaders – the use of bronze. They began to scratch the soil and sow crops. They were joined by the Beaker People, and we know virtually nothing about them except that they made beakers and other vessels.

A new wave of immigrants arrived; the Britons. They were a branch of the Celtic people whose destiny it was to move westward across Europe, or be pushed by other peoples, so that their descendants today are found on the fringes of the Continent – Brittany, Cornwall, Wales, Scotland and Ireland. Their origi-

nal homeland is hardly worth guessing at. They spoke the Celtic tongue, and imposed it on Britain, and they are the people who probably introduced the Iron Age. Welsh is the most direct present-day descendant of the ancient language but there is a Scottish tradition, or myth, that Gaelic, the Scottish form of Celtic, was spoken in the Garden of Eden. Scotland is rich in such myths.

By the beginning of the Christian era, the country had developed a civilisation, united in language. The people worked the land and built little huts clustered in villages, they had horses and wagons, they had quite sophisticated tools. But they were nothing like a nation. There was not enough communication to create anything so integrated. The people (the name Scots itself was not applied until centuries later) were a scatter of tribes keeping themselves to themselves or occasionally quarrelling or forming brief alliances.

Their descendants were to live through an endless series of incursions that would help to bind them together, and the first great threat came from Imperial Rome. It is not easy to understand why the Romans should have wanted to conquer the place, when in Roman terms it was still a scraggy piece of real estate with no wealth and winters designed to freeze the marrow, compared with the genial climate of the Mediterranean and its smiling farms and

Previous page: The standing stones at Callanish in Lewis, the most famous of a number of such stone circles thought to have been set up by the Beaker people between 2000 and 1500 BC. Their purpose and means of construction remain unknown but they may have served as some form of astronomical observatory.

Below: The preserved Stone Age village at Skara Brae on Orkney.

Left: Gold hair ornaments dating from the early part of the first millenium BC, found on Arran.

Second left: A decorated pottery beaker, characteristic of the Beaker People, dating from perhaps 1800 BC and found in a tomb at Jedburgh.

vineyards. But men are driven by strange demons.

Maybe the Roman map of Europe just looked untidy and unfinished with a stretch of terra incognita at the top end of England. It is true too that imperial conquest becomes an insatiable addiction. And perhaps the Emperor was worried that those unknown barbarians to the north of his English settlement might decide some day to surge southward and disturb his Pax Romana.

At any rate, the Emperor Vespasian made the decision in the year 80 AD, and an army under Julius Agricola marched north from England and took over south-east Scotland, without too much difficulty.

It is surprising that they had any difficulty at all. The all-conquering Romans were magnificently disciplined, even brutally disciplined, and steeped in the art of warfare, advancing on this ragged collection of dour barbarians. But the imperial might of Rome was going to have tough and sometimes terrible times before it was finished with Scotland.

In the meantime the push was on, and first central Scotland and then the south-west came under the Roman banner. The hold over the central belt was consolidated with a line of forts from east to west.

The first trouble for the conquerors came with the drive to the north. As a preliminary, the Roman fleet sailed up the east coast to make a show of power and reduce the natives to a trembling respect for the invaders.

The trick had exactly the opposite result. The Caledonians, as Agricola called them, abandoned their neighbourly squabbles and got together to take on the enemy from without. They raided the Roman forts regularly, and if they could not stop the advance they made it a bloody experience.

The Ninth Legion had its first taste of native ferocity in a night raid on its camp. The camp was standard Roman construction. The troops dug a ditch round it and piled the earth as a wall in front, with only a few gaps for access. They posted sentries on the wall and turned in for the night. In the black of night the natives poured through the gaps and over the wall and set about slaughtering the sleeping warriors. The demoralised survivors were fighting for their lives, and not for conquest, when dawn broke and suddenly from the south came a body of Roman cavalry at the gallop. The Scots were caught in a pincer and fell back from the camp, fighting for their own survival. They were beaten, but most of them faded away into the woods, vanished and got ready for another day.

Agricola drove on northward and set up a fortified camp near the head of the Firth (estuary) of the River Tay as a strong point where the fleet could handily deliver food and supplies from the south and free the legions from dependence on the land. From there he carried on the advance to the north.

By this time, probably AD 84, the locals had found a leader, whose name has come down to us in the Latinised form Calgacus; and Calgacus was not overawed by the might of Rome. Somehow, in this thinly populated region, he had rallied, it is said, over thirty thousand fighting men, and this horde was gathered on the hill of Mons Graupius to challenge the advancing legions.

Roman legions had a well-tried process for pitched battles. The well-drilled infantry marched to the attack in line abreast with their

long shields held before them. The front rank would rattle the enemy with a shower of spears and then, if the enemy held their ground, march doggedly forward, stabbing with their swords and literally trampling them into the ground. But it did not work like a machine against this host of thirty thousand. There was a rain of arrows on the leading phalanxes and damage and death on both sides before supporting Romans thundered forward to scatter the defenders. Even then it was all a gory mess as Scottish chariots came ploughing through the ranks, filled with warriors hurling spears and smashing legionaries aside, and the Romans were stopped; and suddenly threatened by masses of Scots pouring down the hill to attack their flanks.

The Romans answered with a massed cavalry charge that sliced through the Scots and then turned to attack again from the rear. There was a fearful slaying and the natives were driven back to the woods. The Romans combed the woods killing or capturing at will. The battle was over.

So was the war, for the moment. The defeated Scots simply left the area and moved to other places. The Pax Romana was established in Scotland, for all the good it did Rome. There was nothing in the place for the Empire except the vanity of victory, and it tied up useful soldiers for years doing nothing much except

show the flag. The garrisons must have spent a lot of time feeling cold and damp and bored and wondering why they had ever joined. And after thirty years of that, the local tribes rediscovered their patriotic enthusiasm. They suddenly attacked the forts and wiped out the bored invaders.

The Ninth Legion now had its second experience of ferocity in Scotland. Probably in the year 118 the legion marched north again to suppress the rebellious ingrates and simply disappeared. No trace has ever been found of the legion or any of its equipment.

Well might the masters of the world, in their kindly climate back on the Tiber, with its good wine and buxom dark-eyed women, have been sick to death of what somebody much later described as the knuckle-end of European civilisation.

But as somebody else, even later, remarked, colonialism is like salted peanuts. You can't stop till you've finished the lot. In the year of AD 122, the Emperor Hadrian visited Britain in person to expunge the insult to the world's Number One power, and he brought enough helpers to guarantee him some respect among the turbulent barbarians.

But he too found that he could see no reason for ruling Scotland. The country could not even produce a decent drink. He decided that England was quite enough, and decided that

Hadrian's Wall, a line of fortresses running across the north of England, would be the limit of Rome's Europe. The Romans would stay to the south of it, and with any luck, the barbarians would stay on the other side and stop being a nuisance.

Many other nations would look at Scotland with greedy eyes. Most of them would end up wishing they had never heard of the place and its troublesome people.

The Romans could not quite give up. In the reign of Antoninus, around the year 142, they climbed over Hadrian's wall and reinforced the dreary old forts built so long ago between the rivers Clyde and Forth. The artefact is called the Antonine Wall, and bits of it can still be traced, though it was made of mere earth and tended to get trodden down as the centuries passed. It was thirty-nine miles long, ten feet high and six feet wide, and now looks like a completely pointless exercise. Legionaries just kept walking back and forth along it, looking out for any sudden upsurge of anti-Roman violence from the north. Most of the time, the Scots left them to this tedious exercise.

Then, in the year 155, the restless natives attacked the thing and chased the Romans. The Scots are widely believed to be stubborn to the point of idiocy. Maybe there was a cross-infection beween them and the Romans, because the Romans returned to the Wall, and the Scots routed them out again. The combination of sheer boredom and commonsense finally persuaded the Empire to leave Scotland to the savages.

Now we come to the dark ages. There are no written records of what Scotland was doing while the Roman Empire still held England for the next two hundred years. But they too got bored, and toward the end of the fourth century

Left: Bust of the Roman Emperor Hadrian.

Below: Many sections of Hadrian's Wall can still be seen, a tribute to the skill of its builders.

they burst out to the south and began the rape of England, where generations of peace had made the inhabitants lax.

The life-style of these northerners was hardly barbarian, but yes, they were barbaric as they ripped down through England. They plundered and burned and destroyed, as far as the English Midlands and nearly to London, and the genial Roman civilisation of England was wiped out, the cornfields reverted to pigs and thistle, and rats and wolves.

The Romans should never have troubled. The Scots are impossible, in the end.

Around the same time, however, there was another invasion of Scotland, another attempt at conquest; not with the sword, but with the Word. The spearhead was the Christian Ninian, a missionary who had visited Rome, and who arrived in Wigtownshire in the south-west at the end of the fourth century to build, at Whithorn, the first Christian church in the country. His followers soon carried on the building programme to the north-east.

It was a very partial conquest. Heathen faiths persisted for centuries. And other, gorier, invaders never gave up. The Angles came from the east, and they succeeded on a bigger scale than Ninian, driving the natives out of the south and east and even out of Scotland altogether.

Above: The outline of a temporary Roman camp can still be clearly seen from the air at Ardoch in Perthshire.

Then there were the Scots, from Ireland – the word Scot itself came with them – and one of them, Fergus, established a little kingdom in Argyllshire on the west coast. The south-west of the country had already been annexed by the Northumbrian king Oswald. The Scots from Ireland had acquired Christianity from Saint Patrick. It did not make them any less aggressive.

And one of the most aggressive arrivals from Ireland was a man whom many people today conventionally imagine as a gentle shepherd. From the time St Columba landed on Iona in 563, he was certainly doing his best to cultivate meekness, compassion and the other Christian virtues. But his previous history was bloody enough for any three men.

Born in County Donegal, he certainly studied the religious life from boyhood, and he was only 25 when he founded the monastery of Derry, and he established another at Durrow in his early thirties. He was nicknamed the Dove, but after what now looks like a trivial quarrel with the Irish king Diarmit over the ownership of a book, he incited some other hotheads to launch an attack on the king at the battle of Cuildremne, which degenerated into a senseless slaughter. The king lost, but in the aftermath of disgust the Dove decided it was best to get away from Ireland.

He was an improbable messenger of peace and love but his sheer energy of temperament was probably an essential part of his mission. The community at Iona, which he shared with twelve followers, was a little church and a group of separate cells for the monks, a few buildings for stores, all enclosed by a turf wall. In his own little cell, the master slept on bare earth with a stone pillow, to seek humility through mortification.

But he left Iona regularly to push back the frontiers of ignorance elsewhere, and on one trip to visit the Pictish king Brude, to plead for the civil rights of the Scots. There are legends of miracles on this visit – one tells that Brude's castle was bolted and barred, but that the doors swung open when Columba touched them with his cross. He seems to have gained the sympathy of the king, though not of his heathen priests. And sailing homewards on Loch Ness, he was able to calm a gale by prayer. The miracles may be exaggerated, but in practical terms the saint was spreading his own little empire up the west coast, and manning little monasteries with fresh recruits from Ireland.

Elsewhere in Scotland, around Glasgow, the Gospel was brought independently by Kentigern. Kentigern was a Briton, and there was very little contact between the two Christian streams, British and Irish or Celtic. There were three cultural strains in Scotland: the Picts, the Scots and the Angles, and religion did very little to bring them together. In future cen-turies, religion was to become a Scottish battlefield.

In the meantime, religion and other traditions in Scotland were under attack again, this time from the Norsemen. They were irresistible. They travelled in long-ships and no other boat could touch them. And again, though Scotland had very little to offer in the way of plunder, the invaders took what they wanted, including the small treasures of the monasteries. They visited Iona twice, bringing destruction and death. It was so easy that they spread their forays into the mainland. These were tireless and ruthless adventurers with an unquenchable appetite for loot and violence. They turned their attention to Ireland and to England and even penetrated right up the Seine, almost as far as Paris. Scotland, a confused collection of rival kinglets, made easy pickings for them. It was not until 843 that the country was united for the first time by Kenneth MacAlpin, a Scot who now ruled both

Below: A sixteenth century impression of a Pictish warrior ready for battle.

Scots and Picts, possibly by force of arms, just as possibly by some ruthless skulduggery.

The unity did not keep the Norsemen out. They took Dumbarton, on the Clyde, and lorded it over the area, and they were the death of three later kings, Constantine, Donald the Second, and Indulf.

They were kings in a time when not many Scottish kings died in their beds. The old turbulence was never far from the surface, and a king was liable to be struggling against the Norsemen, and against new territorial aggression from England, as well as the uncurable rebelliousness of the men of Moray in the

north. It was not until Malcolm II arrived on the throne in 1005 that the country even acquired, at last, a geographical unity with the borders fixed. Malcolm first tried to extend them by occupying the north of England, but had his army cut to pieces and had to slink back to Scotland.

England had other troubles in the shape of the Danes, who had the territory hunger again, and in 1016 the English throne was taken over by Cnut, the man often libelled as believing that the very sea itself respected him so much that the tide would stop rather than soak him. It was his sycophantic courtiers who erected this

Above: The restored church at Iona on the site of St Columba's monastery. Remains of what is believed to be St Columba's own cell and of the graveyard where many early Scottish kings are buried can also be seen nearby.

Opposite: Intricate designs decorate this Pictish symbol stone from Angus.

Left: A monastic cell at Eilach an Naoimh, Argyll. The monastic traditions of the Celtic Church of Ireland were brought to Scotland by St Columba and his followers.

fatuous myth, and Cnut who went to the water's edge to prove what fools they were. Cnut himself was made of stern stuff, and he too had his eye on Scotland, where he considered that the Lothian area belonged to him by right. His forces went to repossess it in 1018, and the Britons and Scots massacred them. Scotland, and her borders, were now stable. Not necessarily forever.

Among the list of kings who followed Malcolm, it is worth mentioning his grandson Duncan, since Shakespeare did. The Shakespeare picture is probably less true to real life than Robert Graves' creation of the emperor Claudius. There was so much tactical and strategic intermarriage among Scottish nobility and royalty that a true and total right to the throne was often very hard to authenticate. Macbeth had royal blood and possibly thought he had a stronger title than Duncan. Macbeth may well have done the dark deed of murder. thus continuing a venerable Scottish tradition. And his conscience doubtless disturbed him, since he went a few years later on a pilgrimage to Rome.

After his return Duncan's son, Malcolm Canmore (Bighead), pursued him from somewhere around Dunsinane and killed him in battle. But Macbeth had held the throne and ruled well for seventeen years, rather more than can be compressed into an evening at the theatre.

The Duncan-Macbeth-Malcolm drama is important, in any case, as a typical manifestation of the times. A student of history who inclined to the romantic is liable to picture those figures of the past as men of heroic stature and nobility, grappling with great affairs and shaping the destiny of the world. Wiser to blow away the mist of time and recognise that men and women are the same in every age, and judge their behaviour as we would judge it if it were here and now.

And on that basis the Homeric figures of the past might often remind us of a group of Mafiosi. Power and the hunger for power are also the same in every age, and in the words of Lord Acton, they tend to corrupt. The plots and counter-plots, the shrewd political marriages, the pitched battles, the seizure of territories, fall into some kind of perspective if we transfer the whole scene to New York, with rival families conniving, making alliances, assassinating, taking over rackets and territories, clawing their way up the ladder to power and property or attaching themselves to the likeliest candidate for leadership.

The main difference is one of scale, since the old kings openly dominated the whole society and not just their underground layer of it. But in both areas, in both ages, most ordinary people go on living their private and social lives and making the best of it, without being constantly aware of being in thrall.

In the meantime, something significant had happened to England: the conquest by the Norman William the Conqueror in 1066. It was to be significant, though the conventional Scottish view of Scottish history has paid little attention to it.

For one thing, it sent hordes of English, and English-speaking refugees fleeing from the North of England into Scotland. With them they brought their language, their particular local version of English. All languages vary from region to region, and theirs was much different from that of London and the South. It was an older form of English, and it established itself in the Lowlands of Scotland. We shall return to this later.

The English refugees included a brother and sister of royal blood; Edgar Atheling and Margaret. To compound the complexities of nationality, they had actually been born in Hungary, and were hoping to get back there, but their ship somehow found itself in the Firth

Above: Great seals of three Scottish kings. Top, left and right, William the Lion (reigned 1165-1214), centre, Alexander II (1214-49), below, Alexander III (1249-85).

Opposite: The Battle of the Standard, fought at Cowton Moor in Yorkshire in 1138 was a serious defeat for the Scots under King David I. Among those fighting for the English against the Scots were ancestors of Robert the Bruce and John Balliol, an illustration of how closely linked were the Anglo-Norman noble families of England and Scotland.

of Forth, which was by no means on the route to Hungary.

Their vessel fetched up in a bay near Dunfermline, in Fife, where King Malcolm had built a royal home for himself. They were met by messengers from the King, who reported back to their master that the girl was of overwhelming beauty. At first sight of her, Malcolm knew he must marry her, and though she had already made up her mind to take the veil, she finally consented.

But she never lost her passion for saintliness, and her king and husband had to put up with it, agreeing to kneel beside her and wash the feet of some emaciated beggar in the name of Christian charity, and provide for her to give out to the poor at religious festivals.

Her saintliness left no room for a sense of humour. She set out to reform the Christian church in Scotland, which had its own customs differing from the rest of Europe. The Scottish version was rather easy-going for her taste, with monks actually marrying, and abbots passing their position down to their sons. There was not too much she could do about it.

On the other hand, she was very enthusiastic about riches and ornamentation, she dressed like a queen and liked other people to do the same. Her king's palace was fabulously decorated with tapestries and furnished with gold and silver plate. In the end, she was the end of Malcolm, since his regard for her fellow-refugees led him into an invasion of England to help them, an invasion which was easily repelled. The Conqueror retaliated with an invasion of Scotland and forced Malcolm to recognise his sovereignty.

William Rufus, who succeeded William the Conqueror, consolidated the English superiority. Malcolm invaded England again in 1093 and was killed in battle at Alnwick.

The saintly Margaret lay ill in Edinburgh when her son Edgar returned and tried to tell her that Malcolm was well. She insisted on the truth, and her saintly response to the news of his death was that her grief was sent to purify her on her deathbed.

Scotland was plunged into its routine struggle among rival successors, including Donald Bane, who managed to seize power for a brief period before William Rufus decided that he preferred the other family, and intervened to secure the Scottish crown for Edgar, the eldest son of Malcolm and Margaret, in 1097.

We have seen the incursion of a form of the English language into Lowland Scotland. It was

Left: St Margaret's Chapel at Edinburgh Castle is the oldest building surviving on the site.

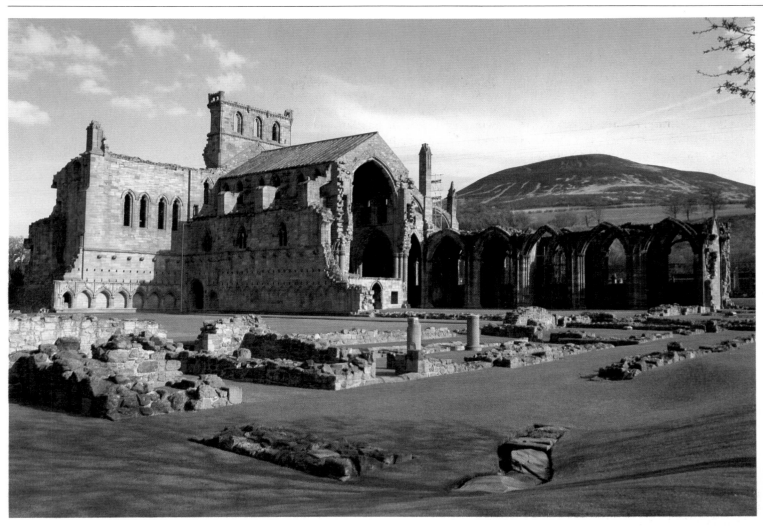

more complicated than that. William the Conqueror himself had had no real interest in taking over Scotland. But the Norman habits he brought with him infiltrated the Scottish nobility almost automatically, just as the Normans supplanted the English nobility.

Norman French was the tongue of the upper classes, the language of the English court, the language to which lesser gentry aspired. And we must realise that during the periods when the Scots and English were not at one another's throats, the upper classes formed a sort of freemasonry. Scottish ladies married English gentlemen, Scottish gentlemen married English ladies, they acquired or inherited lands in both countries. It was not a question of the Scots nobles aping their English betters. They were members of the same club, the same extended tribe. Although they might have notional antagonisms, when kings quarrelled they were not strangers to one another, and the Norman influence was pervasive on the top level. A Breton was appointed Steward of Scotland, and the Stewart dynasty descended from him. There is some controversy about the origin of the word, which is not Norman but Anglo-Saxon. Some scholars hold that it is a version of stig-ward, keeper of the hall; others that it was originally sty-ward, pig-keeper to the king. No matter. Robert the Bruce, the great

Scot of his time, was descended from de Brus, who came over with William the Conqueror and was given a generous gift of Scottish land by King David of Scotland.

Farther down in society, the common people underwent unexpected changes because of the Conquest. When those fugitives from Northern England migrated into the Lowlands, and brought their language, the established Celtic languages of the area retreated before it, and Gaelic retained only a foothold in the High-

Above: Melrose Abbey was founded by grants given by David I (reigned 1124-53). Like many of the border abbeys it often suffered during the wars with England, being finally destroyed by an English invasion in 1544.

Left: A fourteenth century manuscript illustration showing John Balliol acknowledging Edward I of England as his overlord in 1292.

lands and the Islands. Over the centuries it retreated farther until today it is spoken by a mere 100,000 in its own country.

The North of England English dialect that took over was the one that in time became known as Scots, or Scots-English. So modern Scotland has finished up with three languages: Gaelic (which now looks like fighting back and at least consolidating its position); English, or 'Standard' English, written and spoken by educated Scots people in the Lowlands; and Scots, also spoken though seldom written, by many of the same educated Scots people, and certainly spoken by the common Scots people, in town and country, though with enormous variations from area to area.

In the last couple of centuries the Scots have had a slightly shamefaced defensive attitude to the Scots tongue because some of them imagined that it was a corruption of perfect English as spoken by proper people in the south of England.

The truth is that there is no such thing as 'Standard' English. All forms of all languages are merely regional dialects, and most languages are constantly changing in vocabulary and grammar and pronunciation. The Scots tongue is closer to Old English and Middle English than is the speech known to linguists as Southern British Standard, and retains many ancient words long vanished from the southern version. And like Gaelic, it has reasserted its self-confidence in recent decades and can even sometimes be heard on the British Broadcasting Corporation.

For most of the twelfth and thirteenth centuries, then, the English penetration was peaceable. Scotland was still divided all the same, since the Western Isles were in the hands of the Norwegian kings, and when King Magnus looked like pushing into the mainland too, in 1098, the Scots king David agreed formally to cede the Western Isles to Norway for the sake of peace. The contract was that Magnus was to hold thrall over every island

that could be circumnavigated by a fully equipped longship. By a nice piece of legalistic chicanery Magnus took over a mainland peninsula, the Mull of Kintyre, by having a boat dragged across the isthmus.

As the years went by the Norsemen regularly behaved like Norsemen, raiding the lowlands and even penetrating to Glasgow in one series of forays before they were pushed back. In 1263 the long bitterness finally came to a head when a new Norwegian king, Haakon, brought a huge fleet from Scandinavia, to consolidate his grip on the islands and have a try for the whole of Scotland too.

He was beaten, appropriately enough, by the Scottish climate. The fleet sailed round the southern tip of the Mull and right up the Firth of Clyde. The Scots king, Alexander III, shrewdly played for time by sending envoys to discuss a treaty. Nothing came of it. Nothing was meant to come of it. The autumn was wearing on, and Alexander was praying for a gale; which he got. It was the prevailing sou-westerly, and it roared across the Firth so violently that a dozen of Haakon's ships were blown aground on the mainland at the village of Largs, where the Scots were waiting.

There was a rather scrappy to-and-froing for a couple of days. The Scots archers ran short of arrows and resorted to heaving stones at the enemy, Largs beach being composed of stones of just the right size. The Scottish cavalry arrived, and its effect was mostly psychological, but the invaders were suitably impressed and found their way back to their ships any way they could. The Battle of Largs is still remembered locally as a heroic event. It was in truth a messy affair won by luck as well as valour. But a few years later, Alexander agreed to pay a new Norwegian king a ransom which brought the Hebrides back into the Scottish kingdom; but not very far back. The Hebrideans paid very little attention to the kings of Scotland, who wisely left them very much alone.

Left: The royal seal of King John Balliol showing the king in the normal poses of military leader and judge or lawgiver.

Another nice irony was the death of Alexander, which was accomplished by a combination of his own stubbornness and that old Scottish climate. Some hysteric or other had prophesied the Day of Judgement. A terrible storm blew. Alexander decided to cross the Firth of Forth in a little ferry-boat, to defy judgement. His battered body was found washed up on the shore. And suddenly, the old Scottish-English confrontation was back.

There was King Edward I of England, brother-in-law and friend to the dead Scottish king. Alexander's only descendant was a little girl of three, the daughter of his son-in-law King Eric of Norway. The girl herself died in childhood, and Edward saw the way to taking over Scotland.

. In the general confusion among the Scottish nobles, he was invited to choose among the conflicting claims, and he picked John Balliol. The price, to Balliol, was that he had to offer allegiance to Edward, which seemed all right to Balliol. But Edward set out to make it plain that Balliol was under his orders. Balliol acquired the nickname Toom Tabard – empty coat; a showpiece king with no substance inside the royal robes. When Balliol rebelled at being treated as a lackey, Edward marched on Scotland, right to the north, and took over the country as an English colony.

During the ups and downs of these campaigns, there was one Robert de Brus, grandson of one of Balliol's rivals, who could not quite decide what was best for him. He sometimes put himself forward as a passionate Scot, at other times spoke up for King Edward – waiting to see how the dice would fall. One man whose mind was totally made up was William Wallace, or Sir William Wallace, a mere boy in his twenties in the town of Paisley; a fairly violent youth with a lot of blood on his hands, but a complete conviction that he was Scottish, Edward was English, and Scotland must be free of the king they called the Hammer of the Scots.

Wallace raised an enthusiastic army – not a high-class army, because he was of obscure descent and beneath the notice of the Scottish barons. He was just a very good soldier. He tramped his men into the north and retook the castles that Edward had captured. The Scots were on the march. Their first big victory was in September 1297 at Stirling Bridge.

This battle demonstrated the military brilliance of Wallace. After a few absurd manoeuvres, the enemy marched northwards across the bridge, without opposition. Then Wallace's men sprang up from nowhere to attack the leaders, while others poured on to the bridge to cut the rearguard to pieces. The

Above: Wallace's stunning victory at Stirling Bridge in 1297. King Edward's lieutenant in Scotland, the Earl of Surrey, fled to England. Wallace became Guardian of Scotland, ruling in the name of King John Balliol, by then imprisoned in England.

English survivors fled. Wallace was the master of Scotland.

Unfortunately, the Scottish aristocracy refused to recognise this low-born upstart, and when Edward came north for revenge, it was a poor little band that Wallace had under his command when he faced the Hammer at Falkirk in 1298. The Scots were overwhelmed. In 1305 Wallace, a hunted man, was betrayed and carried to London to be charged with treason. He rejected the charge, since he had never given his loyalty to an English king. He was hanged, drawn and quartered all the same.

And so came the next ambitious Scot, or adoptive Scot, to fight for independence. Robert the Bruce, the Earl of Carrick in Ayrshire, had been a trusted ally of Edward. What he wanted was to be king of Scotland. Seeing a possible rival in the Earl of Badenoch – 'the Red Comyn' – he invited him to a church in Dumfries, and in a fit of temper stabbed him; a desecration for which Bruce was excommunicated, and lost much of the support of the Scottish nobles. Nonetheless Bruce quickly had himself crowned king at Scone in March 1306.

The simple throne on which he was crowned did not contain the Stone of Destiny, a massive slab which according to legend had come from

Above: The Bruce monument at Bannockburn, scene of his greatest triumph.

Above left: Isabella, Countess of Buchan, was imprisoned by Edward I at Berwick Castle from 1306-13 because she had participated in Bruce's coronation. She was from the family of the Earls of Fife who had the hereditary right to crown the Scottish king. The painting is by the Dundee artist Stewart Carmichael and dates from 1908.

Left: King Robert the Bruce presenting a charter to the burgesses of Edinburgh in 1329, from a painting by William Hole.

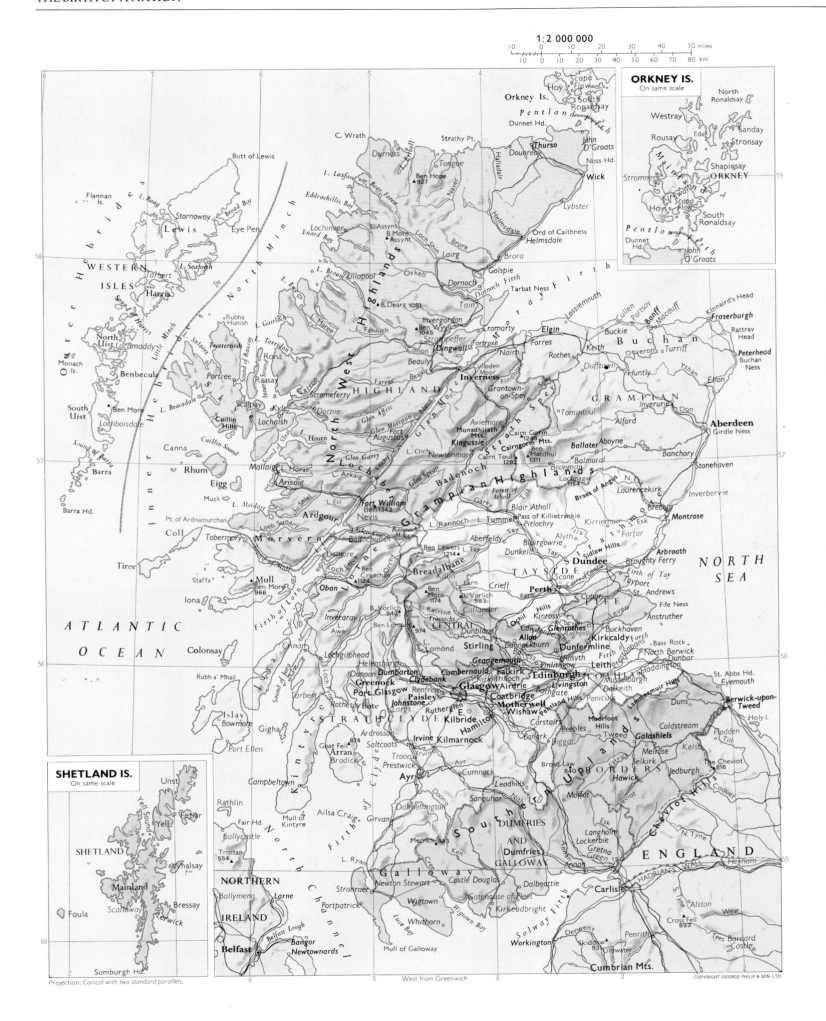

1 : 2 000 000

Projection: Conical with two standard parallels.

West from Greenwich

COPYRIGHT. GEORGE PHILIP & SON. LTD.

ROBERTVS I. REX SCOTORVM M CCC VI ANNO DOM

Left: King Robert the Bruce. Although he had fought both with and against Edward of England, Bruce is commonly remembered today as an undoubted Scottish patriot.

Right: The famous incident on the eve of Bannockburn when the lightly-armed King Robert nimbly avoided the charge of Henry de Bohun and felled him with a blow from his axe.

the Holy Land and had pillowed Jacob's Head. Scottish kings were traditionally crowned above this legendary rock; but it had already been stolen by Edward of England during his conquest and taken to Westminster in London.

(There is a 20th century postscript to that story. In 1950, on Christmas Eve, a small group of bold, or reckless, Scottish Nationalists recaptured the Stone from Westminster Abbey and took it back to Scotland, in a symbolic bid to restore the country's independence. It was recovered and taken back to London 14 months later, but to many Scots the exploit is still remembered as an heroic feat, or at the very least a splendid joke.)

Despite his coronation Bruce was soon in trouble, attacked by Edward's men and forced

to flee Scotland and hide on the island of Rathlin, off the Irish coast. But whatever his motives, he was a man of unquenchable courage, and a titanic fighter, capable of taking on three or four attackers and dispatching them with the broadsword. He gathered supporters in Scotland after his exile. It may well be that his misery on Rathlin was cured by the sight of a spider that would not give up trying to swing to a distant cave wall. There is nothing wrong with legends. The fact is that Bruce tried and tried again, and conquered most of Scotland.

The climax was Bannockburn, which has engraved the date 1314 on the heart of Scottish patriots ever since. The English mustered 20,000 men, Bruce had 6000 and an inflexible determination. And it produced another legi-

One of Bruce's individual feats of showy valour.

And his strategy worked as well. The English were finished convincingly. The defeated King Edward II of England, a less effective leader than his dreaded father, could not quite admit that he was finished. There were further raids across the border, answered by invasions into England by Bruce. Edward III finally agreed to be done with colonial ambitions, and the Treaty of Northampton in 1328 recognised the independence of Scotland and the kingship of Bruce.

A death mask of the king of Scots reveals the symptoms of the leprosy that afflicted him in his later years. By then it was not the scourge it had been before and since; at that time, the strain was weak and lepers were not uncommon in Scotland, going about their lives without straining themselves or frightening others. But no doubt it contributed to his early death in 1329. Shortly before it, the Pope revoked the sentence of excommunication.

After the Bruce, Scotland would go on having troubles and strife; but as an independent and even united nation, not to be overwhelmed by an act of war. By other acts more subtle, perhaps.

Below: A Victorian engraving shows Bruce giving orders to an unlikely army of kilted spearmen. Nonetheless Bruce's army was drawn in large part from the Highlands.

timate legend when, on the evening before the main battle, an English knight, Henry de Bohun, rode out to do battle with an obscure Scottish horseman, charged him with lance in position, only to see the Scot's horse swerve; the last thing he saw, since the Scot swung his battle-axe and split de Bohun's head in two.

2 The Stewarts

THE PEACE was too flimsy to last. Edward III of England had not really lost his appetite for Scotland. He was aggrieved that several Scottish estates had not been returned to his own barons who had held the estates before the Treaty of Northampton, and decided that this amounted to a breach of the treaty.

Or so he claimed. Land in Scotland was not worth a great deal, but people in high places still had their incurable hunger for it. Edward encouraged Edward Balliol, son of the pathetic John Balliol (Toom Tabard), to invade, with the bait of kingship, and in 1332, just four years after the agreement of everlasting peace between the kingdoms, Balliol and his men arrived in Fife by sea and approached a hastily patched-up Scottish army under the Earl of Mar.

Mar was no master of war, his sentries were inadequate, and the invaders struck without warning and conducted a massacre at Dupplin Moor in Perthshire. Balliol had himself crowned in Perth and then travelled round the country to demonstrate his power. Unluckily a small band of Scots attacked him as he slept in Annan, and he was lucky to get to his horse and escape to England.

He returned, with the help of Edward in person, and Edward himself came back regularly to take over the Scottish strongholds and attempt to consolidate his power as the real ruler of the country.

The power soon crumbled. The Scots, knowing from experience that they were inferior to the English in battle, adopted the system of simply fading out of sight, taking their beasts and leaving the land to rot. And by 1339 Edward had bigger things on his mind, his invasion of France that was to launch the ludicrous Hundred Years' War. Deprived of his support, the English fortresses in Scotland were recaptured one by one.

Another minor confusion of the time is that Robert Bruce had contracted what was to be a long-lasting alliance with France, 'The Auld Alliance', two years before the Treaty of Northampton. It was not always to Scotland's advantage. The French, quite reasonably, saw that if the English were harried from the North, they would be distracted from their operations on the Continent, and when the Scots obliged with minor invasions of England they were usually routed. In one of them, in 1346, King David II marched on the old enemy, was utterly defeated and taken to London as a prisoner. He was not released until 1357, for a huge ransom.

David, the last of the Bruces, was a pathetic shadow of the original liberator. Possibly his years of fairly comfortable imprisonment in England had even destroyed his taste for Scotland and the Scots. He actually suggested that if he died childless, one of Edward's sons should succeed him. The Scottish nobles threw the

suggestion out without discussion. And when he did die, in 1371, the man who followed him was Robert the Steward, son of Walter, Robert Bruce's son-in-law.

Robert II, as he became, the first of the Stewarts, was also no firebrand, and he ruled, or made a show of ruling, over a Scotland that was again dominated by squabbling barons who thought little of him. He was dragged reluctantly into yet another invasion of England by the arrival of a French force, but left it to William Earl of Douglas to take charge of the operation, which achieved nothing except a counter-attack by John of Gaunt and wholesale destruction in Scotland itself.

James, the next Earl of Douglas, chose the heroic role, and took a force into England in 1388, which performed little more than a few showy skirmishes, but did capture the banner of Sir Henry Percy, the celebrated Hotspur, who obeyed his own nature and pursued the Scots in a fury. The two little armies came together at Otterburn, where Percy at first successfully attacked the Scottish camp at nightfall, but was suddenly assaulted on the flank by a small force led by Douglas. The fight lasted all night, with victory to the Scots.

ROBERT II.

Above: King Robert II, the first of the Stewarts, a timid and kind-hearted man trying to rule a turbulent kingdom. His legacy of more than a dozen sons and numerous daughters meant that in succeeding years there would be all too many claimants to his throne.

Previous page: Linlithgow Palace was considerably extended by James IV.

The legend (true this time) is that some time during the night, Douglas was mortally wounded and realised his death might demoralise his men. But he lived long enough to tell his neighbours to keep the thing secret, to wave his banner and cry 'A Douglas!' The scheme worked and the battle was won.

Again it must be remembered that although this is the stuff of which history is made, it is the very small stuff, deceptively enlarged by the passing of time; an incident in a long period of petulant quarrels like magnified street fights.

And after the death of Robert II, the endemic squabbles went on, in a nation that was administratively a mess. The new monarch, Robert III, was half-crippled from a riding accident, and temperamentally unfitted either to war or to government, things he left to other more active or more ambitious men. He ruled nominally for only fourteen years, from 1390 to 1406, and what happened in Scotland, and to Scotland, in that time, had little to do with him, and more to do with his vigorous brother the Duke of Albany.

The Highland clans were as turbulent as always, fighting among themselves and raiding the lowlands as cattle rustlers, a trade invented in Scotland long before the American West was won. Sir David Lindsay was the man charged with repelling the ferocious Gaels. He had another of those wild theatrical Scottish ideas, and proposed a battle of champions between the two most hostile clans to settle the trouble; and the clans were wild enough to take to the notion. Each sent thirty fighting men to battle on the North Inch, an island in the River Tay at Perth, and hordes of local people joined the king for the enjoyment of a slaughter suitable for a Roman arena. When it was over 53 of the combatants were gorily dead. Two survived on one side, and five on the other. And of course, the great circus, though it provided merry sport for the citizens of Perth, left the Highlands as troublesome as ever.

Robert's reign was latterly shadowed, too, by more of the murky and complex family affairs that were the passionate pastime of the Scottish nobility. His drunken son the Duke of Rothesay was promised in a strategic marriage to the daughter of the Earl of March, but the Earl of Douglas put pressure on Robert to have the prince marry his own daughter, and Robert agreed. This becomes more and more mysterious when we find that the fiancé so much in demand now vanishes from the face of the

Below: A nineteenth century impression of the Battle on the North Inch at Perth in 1396 between the picked warriors of the clans Chattan and Kay. King Robert III and his court are interested spectators.

Eft
reny d
honur
mat d
Enesp
y Xu
grauc
war
pieces
Enesp
ler

robt de Frekyn z william de lenyn
Robt Seneschall Gardein destorer Prelat
ne q traittie z accorde est parentie les
re soit franchement deliurez hors de p
gent sur les condicions z en manere
kyngs a pater deseinz eys aus prochex
Teftassinoir les tres ank mares du pri

articlis puns

Left: The Battle of Homildon in 1402 was as much part of a family feud between the English Percy clan and the Scottish Douglases as an episode in an international war. Archibald, 4th Earl of Douglas was the loser on this occasion and was captured by Henry Percy (Hotspur). Both feature in Shakespeare's *Henry IV*.

Opposite: A fourteenth century manuscript shows David II during his captivity at the English court. He is seen shaking hands with Edward III of England.

Below: James I, painted here by an unknown artist, spent most of his childhood as a prisoner in England and did not return to rule Scotland until he was 30. He proved an able king but made powerful enemies which led to his murder in 1437.

earth. One presumption is that he was imprisoned in Falkland Castle and left to starve to death, by his uncle the Duke of Albany and by Douglas. Douglas's complicity seems bizarre and improbable, but it was a bizarre and improbable age.

In the meantime, the disappointed and outraged Earl of March had washed his hands of the vacillating king and went to England to throw in his lot with Henry IV.

Henry had domestic troubles on his hands too, with a nation bubbling with dissension, but Hotspur was available, and not friendly to the Scots. The new young Earl of Douglas — again, not a patch on his father — led a little army into Northumberland, advanced on Hotspur's forces, and with what may have been simple cowardice, stopped and waited to see what would happen. What happened was that Hotspur's men took the Scottish invaders by storm.

King Robert was dying in 1406, a widower with one young child, James, and no sign of peace except the peace of the grave. He had the boy sent to France for safety. The ship, and the boy, were captured by the English. His father died on the same day.

Albany found himself in sole charge of Scotland, as far as any man could be in charge, and he was content to leave his king imprisoned in London. The Scottish people lived lives of varying hardship in a country that had spent too much of its time in martial adventures to develop prosperous agriculture or anything else, and the clan invasions and the baronial feuds were the facts of recorded history. When

IACOBVS I·D·GRATIA REX·SCOTORVM

Albany died in 1420 his son Murdach inherited his power, and it was not until four years later that James was freed by the English.

Here was a man with some of the qualities of a ruler, and some qualities unexpected in a king. He was an athlete, he had ambition and resolution, but he was also a poet and a musician, and interested in machinery. Above all, he was a passionate patriot, and he dreamed of making his country peaceful and prosperous. He was also married to Joan, grand-daughter of John of Gaunt, which could be politically useful in future relations with England.

Law and order, and respect for it, were his platform. And he was in a hurry. After his coronation at Perth he convened a reorganised Parliament and pushed through legislation which proscribed private wars and enacted for rebellion not only the death penalty, but seizure of the offenders' property. High-born citizens who failed to offer help in crushing rebellion faced the same sanctions. The long-established practice of the nobles of side-tracking rents rightfully due to the throne was forbidden.

James settled on Perth as the royal seat, and ordained an annual meeting of Parliament there. And in the 1425 Parliament, to show that he meant business, he arraigned the mighty Duke of Albany for treason. A court of his peers returned a verdict of guilty and the great man was executed, along with his two sons. At a later Parliament, in Inverness, James extended the same draconian treatment to the Highlands. As they arrived the chieftains were seized and imprisoned, and a number of them were executed or exiled.

These were notable if barbaric achievements, and the retaliation was barbaric too. His own chamberlain, Sir Robert Stewart, prepared a plot that was to mature at Blackfriars Monastery, where the king was spending Christmas of 1436. He was spending a pleasant evening talking to Queen Joan and her ladies-in-waiting when a scream warned them of danger. The bolt had been secretly taken from the door of his room, but one of the Queen's ladies rushed to put her arm through the staples to delay the intruders while the King hid in a cellar. The intruders forced open the door, breaking the girl's arm – another legend, Kate Bar-lass.

Below: The murder of James I, from the painting by Opie. James might have escaped his attackers through a drain leading below the room but the end had been blocked because it interfered with the royal tennis court.

Her courage was futile. The king was found, downed two of his attackers, but was overcome and stabbed to death.

His unfortunate heir, James II, was a boy only six years of age.

He was to grow into a tough and forceful ruler, but in the meantime the country was again a prize to be tussled over by rival nobles. One of them, Crichton, solved his own problem by having another, the young Earl Douglas, murdered at dinner in Edinburgh Castle, in the presence of the protesting boy king. As he grew up, James developed a slightly suspicious friendship with the kinsman who succeeded to the Douglas title; more and more suspicious as Douglas seemed to be

implicated in fresh trouble in the Highlands. And finally there was a gruesome repetition of a previous scene when the king invited Douglas to dine in Stirling Castle, and told him he must sever his connection with the rebellious Lord of the Isles. Douglas refused contemptuously to give his promise, and James himself pulled out a dagger and stabbed him.

In the weird but predictable manner of the time, James found himself virtually at war with the new heir to the Douglas title, but later appointed him ambassador to England – and still later found that Douglas conspiring with the Lord of the Isles and others to unseat him. He sought the advice of a man presumably above political ambition, Bishop Kennedy of St

Above: The coronation of the six-year-old King James II at Holyrood took place within five weeks of his father's murder.

Above: The seal of the Royal Burgh of Rutherglen, one of the oldest royal burghs in Scotland. The earliest known use of the seal is in 1357, though the burgh is certainly older. The devices on the seal are a galley, representing Rutherglen's status as a port on the Clyde, and the Virgin Mary holding the Christ child.

Left: James III symbolically receives his crown from St Andrew, from *The Trinity Altarpiece* by van der Goes from the former Holy Trinity Church, Edinburgh. The third figure may be the king's son, the future James IV, or perhaps one of the king's brothers. The Holy Trinity Church was demolished in 1848 to make way for the present Waverley Station.

Andrews, and the tale is that the Bishop invited him to break a tied bundle of arrows across his knee. It could not be done. The Bishop then untied the bundle and broke the arrows one by one.

The king took the hint, and set about separating Douglas's accomplices from the Earl, attacking them and executing the losers, and Douglas had to leave the country for his safety. But like so many Scottish Kings, James was not destined to die in his bed. Civil war broke out in England, and in 1460 he took advantage of it to recapture Roxburgh, which had long been possessed by the English. Fascinated, like his father, by machines, he tried his hand at operating a siege gun, and it blew up and killed him, leaving Scotland to another boy king, James III, and another instalment in the long story of baronial in-fighting.

He survived it, and in his teens shrewdly married Princess Margaret of Denmark, which brought the Orkney and Shetland Islands into the kingdom. But James found very little peace and never succeeded in winning over the truculent barons. He found that they were not interested in peace, but in dethroning him and replacing him with his brother Alexander, the Duke of Albany. James put Albany in prison, but Albany escaped to France and then England. He moved back to Scotland in 1482, this time leading a force provided by the English King Edward IV, who had revived the ancient ambition of putting a puppet king in Scotland and ruling over it.

James had few allies and plenty of enemies, and he found himself confined in Edinburgh

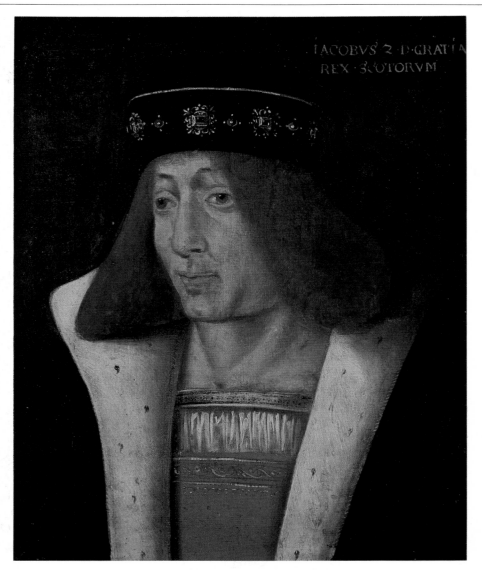

IACOBVS 2 D·GRATIA REX · SCOTORVM

Castle while his brother ruled as regent – and found exactly the same trouble and hostility among the nobles as the king had, and left for England again. For a time James was able to establish his kingly power, but a fresh revolution dethroned him and put his son James in his place.

The King managed to raise an army among the northern barons, and forced a negotiated peace which rapidly evaporated, and the king's men were defeated at Sauchieburn in Stirlingshire in 1488. The prince, on the side of the rebels, had a bad conscience about his part in it. It was worsened when the murdered body of his father was found a few days later. He had given orders that no one should offer violence to the king. He swore to wear a penitential chain round his body as long as he lived.

In spite of that, what was most obvious about James IV was his taste for merriment and high living. His father had been stingy. He was splendidly extravagant, and his subjects liked him for it, he wore gorgeous clothes, he enjoyed gambling, and he gave generously to beggars. Aside from that, he did rule Scotland, and brought law and order into a large part of it. The travelling law courts were tightened up,

Above: James II, 1430-60 (reigned 1437-60) as painted by an unknown artist.

Left: A page from a fourteenth century manuscript, the Murthly Hours. Notes hand-written on the book are believed to be the second oldest example existing of written Gaelic.

and in time he even subdued the men of the Isles. There were, naturally, further occasional skirmishes with the English, they were virtually a law of nature. But there was hope there too when James married Margaret Tudor, daughter of Henry VII, in 1503.

Scotland was at peace and in relative prosperity. The king had a new treaty of perpetual amity with England and renewed the alliance with France too. He established a respectable navy and had the respect of other monarchs. By all the normal criteria, James IV was a good king.

Something went wrong, something familiar went wrong. France found itself in conflict with the Holy League, which included England, and appealed for help. It was a combined appeal by Louis and his Queen, Anne, and Anne was clever enough to appeal to James's chivalry. He rejected wise advice and rallied his nobles for a direct attack on England.

It was a fine large army he led for the invasion. It was also a fine army that moved north to meet it under the command of Lord Thomas Howard. The Scots were massed on Flodden Hill, and instead of attacking directly, Howard made a wide circle and approached the Scots from the north. When they exchanged preliminary gunfire, the English fire was enormously more effective, and when the two forces came together, it seemed for a while like an equal struggle, but the English arms were more efficient and more deadly, and they took a hideous toll. Thirteen Scottish earls were killed, and so was King James. And his heir was a boy hardly over a year old.

Above: King James IV, from a painting in the Scottish National Portrait Gallery by an unknown artist. A long description of James by a Spanish diplomat survives in which James is portrayed as an able and hard-working ruler, pious and humane, but a rash and foolhardy general.

Left: The famous cannon *Mons Meg* photographed in Edinburgh Castle in 1888. Mons Meg is believed to have been imported by James III. Artillery was enormously expensive, beyond the pocket of any but the king, but it gave the king a weapon that enabled him, if necessary, to capture any noble's stronghold.

Left: Illustration from a tract describing the Scottish defeat at Flodden. James IV's able rule and popularity helped him raise a large and well-equipped army which was defeated largely because of his poor generalship.

In the routine jockeying for power, one of the favourites was the Earl of Angus, another Douglas, who married the widowed Queen in 1514, a year after Flodden, and the Earl of Arran was a powerful contender. But another Stewart appeared, from France, John the Duke of Albany, whose father had tried to seize the throne for himself. Albany took over as Governor, but did very little that was constructive, and being thoroughly French had very little interest. There was an abortive rebellion in the Border country, and when Albany took a long vacation in France there was even a skir-mish in Edinburgh, between Angus, who had control of the castle and the king, and the Earl of Arran, who wanted both. The Angus group won, but over seventy were killed on both sides before Arran fled.

The king was both a schoolboy and a pampered prisoner, and neither condition pleased him. He fled from Falkland Palace and had no difficulty in recruiting a little army of people who hated Angus. It never came to a fight. Angus left for England rather than risk it, and the teenage boy very cheerfully took on the duties of monarchy.

Left: The young King James V arrives at Stirling in 1528 following his escape from captivity with the Douglas family.

Left: William Hole's evocative painting *News of Flodden*. The calamity of Flodden was probably the worst ever Scottish defeat in the wars with England and is remembered in the famous lament *The Floo'ers of the Forest*.

James V was the king who roamed the country posing as a commoner, the Gudeman of Ballangeich, to find out what made his ordinary subjects tick. He also had a great enthusiasm for law and order. He was tired of the Borderers who made a trade, a way of life, out of pillage, and took a hunting party to Gilnockie to winkle out the most notorious of them, Johnny Armstrong. Armstrong, king of his own castle, mistook the arrival for a friendly visit, and rode out with a little band of his rowdies to say a polite hello to the boy. James coolly ordered his men to seize the Armstrongs and hang them at once.

He was as keen as his father had been on a properly organised process of justice, and set

Right: King James V, 1512-42, painted here by an unknown artist, succeeded in considerably increasing the royal revenue but was never a genuinely popular or successful king.

IACOBVS 5 D GRA
REX SCOTORVM

PATRICIUS
HAMILTON

Crudeli Morte
Punitus Feb. 1527

Left: Patrick Hamilton was not the first heretic to be burned in Scotland; a Lollard refugee from England had been martyred during the minority of James I a hundred years before but Hamilton was the first who is known to have been a native Scot. Although an annotation on the painting shows Hamilton as dying in 1527 in fact he was killed in 1528.

up a College of Justice, the Court of Session, fifteen qualified men to judge in civil cases and sit all year round in Edinburgh, as a replacement for the old Committee of Causes which had met only during the annual meeting of Parliament. The money to finance the court was to be raised by taxing the Scottish bishops and abbots, with the permission of the Pope, but James used most of it for other purposes. Nonetheless the court prospered. Seven of the judges were laymen, and eight clergymen. Catholic clergymen, of course. This is worth noting because already there were forces filtering in from Europe which would have their effect on that. The Protestant crusade of Martin Luther had already swept over the north of the Continent. In England, for reasons that had nothing to do with theology but a lot to do with money, Henry VIII had rejected the

authority of the Pope, established himself as the head of the church in England, and mopped up the rich spoils of the monasteries.

In Scotland, even some devout Catholics were unhappy about the wealth, the worldly wealth of bishops and abbots, and their lives of luxurious indolence. Other Scots were prepared to challenge the doctrines of the church, and Papal authority, and in James's own time they provided their first martyr in Patrick Hamilton, a student who embraced the Lutheran precept that people must live their lives not by order of the church and mediaeval theology, but by the Bible and each individual's reading of it. Banished for his dangerous statements, Hamilton met Luther, and came back even more articulate and fearless.

He came back, to be exact, to St Andrews University, sure and confident in his faith, but

Left: Mary of Guise, mother of Mary Queen of Scots, in a painting attributed to Corneille de Lyon. Mary ruled as Regent during her daughter's minority.

he was constantly spied on, and in 1528 James Beaton, Archbishop of St Andrews had him arrested, convicted him of heresy and ordered him to be burned alive. He lived for six hours in the flames without ever recanting.

History became entangled with religion. The martyrdom of Hamilton achieved what martyrdom often does, it horrified Scots with gentle hearts and provoked curiosity about the forbidden doctrine. And in England, Henry VIII, though he had no quarrel with Catholic dogma, could see the point of a Protestant Reformation in Scotland as a means of developing an anti-Papal alliance, in which Scotland would be the junior partner, to be absorbed by the senior partner. He insistently invited James to come to England to discuss a strategy for seizing the monasteries. Instead, James went to Catholic France to find a wife, Princess Made-

leine, and when she died young, sent to Catholic France for his second, Mary of Guise.

Bowing to history, Henry sent an invasion fleet and an army to get his will by traditional methods. They succeeded in doing some damage, but proved nothing. King James sent a force across the border, a rather pointless exercise. It was trapped and captured in the marshes of Solway Moss by the English, in a rather pointless battle in November 1542.

James was a sick man, lying in Falkland Palace, when news came from Linlithgow that the queen had had a child; a daughter. The Stewart dynasty had begun with the marriage of Marjorie Bruce to Walter the Steward. The king looked bleakly at the messenger and uttered the not quite prophetic words: 'It cam' wi' a lass, it'll gang wi' a lass.' And lay back to die.

3 Reformation and the English Union

WITH THE arrival of Mary, the story of the Stewarts, and of Scotland, takes a new turn. The tale is no less charged with treachery and blood, and again it sees the country being torn between France and England. But for all the confusion of strife, it is aiming in a new direction. It is confused by what amounts to a civil religious war; but it is moving.

At the centre was the completely passive figure of the newborn infant queen. At the outer edges were the kings of England and France, both, by this time, hungering after the possession of Scotland. Henry VIII was certainly afflicted with that age-old obsession, that *vice anglais* of English monarchs. He foresaw a bloodless conquest through the simplest old royal trick, having his son Edward marry the Scottish infant, who was Henry's great-niece.

It went marvellously smoothly; often a bad omen in Scottish history. The Scottish government agreed, by the Treaty of Greenwich in 1543, to the betrothal of their year-old queen. Almost immediately, of course, they thought better of it having guessed at the English motives. Under the Earl of Arran, they repudiated the Treaty a few months later, and it was war again.

An English fleet arrived off Leith in 1544 under the Earl of Hertford, sacked the town and advanced on the defenceless Edinburgh. Within a few days of pillage and arson the capital city was destroyed. But there was no surrender of the castle itself. The Scots rallied and at Ancrum Moor the next year routed an English force. The Earl of Hertford came back, by land, to burn and loot the borders. And more and more of the Scottish leaders found themselves looking towards France as a friend in need.

As always, they were in two minds. France remained a bastion of the old Roman Catholic faith, while the new Protestant idea was winning over more and more of the Scots nobles, even if they did not flaunt their heresy.

One of the most powerful Scots, and staunchest in the Roman faith was Cardinal David Beaton, Archbishop of St Andrews, who equally hated the English and the Scottish Protestants; and in particular George Wishart, who preached the new faith quite recklessly and survived an attempted assassination. With Wishart as he stumped the country was John Knox, a burly bearded dominie, carrying a broadsword to protect the preacher.

Knox was not visible when Wishart was arrested, because Wishart had ordered his

Previous page: Inchmahome Priory on an island in the Lake of Menteith, the childhood home of Mary Queen of Scots.

Left: George Wishart, c1513-46, who had been a student at St Andrews before studying in England and Switzerland. He returned to Scotland and preached to large congregations before being arrested and burned for heresy.

Below: Wishart Preaching against Mariolatry by Douglas. Mariolatry or excessive veneration of the Virgin Mary was opposed by the Protestant reformers as detracting from true worship according to scripture and distancing man from God.

protector to disappear rather than be captured too, and possibly killed. It was a wise and kindly thought, because Beaton judged Wishart guilty of heresy and ordered him burned alive before St Andrews Castle. According to the accounts, Wishart showed the calm courage of the true martyr as the flames destroyed him.

Beaton himself did not have the stuff of martyrs. When a body of Wishart's followers burst into the Castle a few weeks later on the trail of revenge, he wailed, 'I am a priest, I am a priest, you will not slay me.' A blow from a sword felled him and he died whimpering. The Protestants took over the Castle, and their power made St Andrews a haven for dissidents. John Knox found his power as a preacher, and was able to preach undisturbed.

The haven was temporary, and so was Knox's freedom. In 1547 the Scots had the novel experience of an invasion from France, by a ship that sailed into St Andrews Bay and bombarded the Castle. A landing party dragged great guns into the town to step up the

Left: Cardinal-Archbishop David Beaton of St Andrews, murdered three months after he had Wishart burned.

Left: The burning of Wishart, from an early engraving. Wishart only returned to Scotland from exile in 1543 or 1544 so his active preaching career was short but his influence was substantial.

attack, destroyed the Castle walls and seized the defenders, who were shipped to France as galley slaves.

Rather more routine, another invasion from England, led again by Hertford, now Duke of Somerset and de facto ruler, Protector, of England, during the boyhood of Edward VI. He led a land and sea force in 1547 into the Firth of Forth and closed with the Scots army at Pinkie, a few miles east of Edinburgh. After a savage resistance, the Scots were overcome and killed in hundreds.

Above: The painting by James Drummond entitled *George Wishart on his way to Execution Administering the Sacrament for the First Time in Scotland after the Protestant Form.* According to the teachings of the Protestant reformers the sacraments of the church were to be limited to baptism and communion.

Left: St Andrews Castle was held by Beaton's murderers and other supporters of Wishart for a year but fell after the arrival of a French fleet.

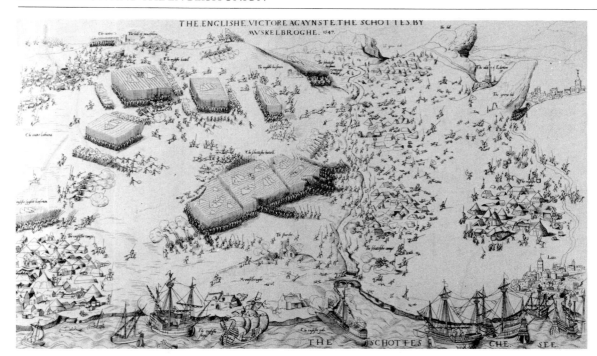

THE ENGLISHE VICTORE AGAYNSTE THE SCHOTTES BY MVSKELBROGHE. 1547

Left: The Battle of Pinkie in September 1547 was a decisive English victory but brought no lasting success.

Other English forces took Broughty Castle on the River Tay, captured Haddington and carried on the trade of looting. But now the Auld Alliance worked in Scotland's favour, and with the help of an army from France the Scots recaptured the prizes and chased the English. The infant queen was taken to France, to be married in time to the Dauphin, and from that time Henry of France steadily tightened his grip on Scotland, not so much as an ally, but more as an emperor.

By the time she came to be married, at the age of fifteen, the beautiful redhead Queen of Scots put her country in pawn to him for a million crowns – notionally the cost of her upbringing – and made a will bequeathing Scotland to Henry if she died without an heir. The eight

Scottish envoys who had been invited to the ceremony at Notre Dame knew nothing of this. For that matter, four of them fell suddenly ill and died before they left France.

In the meantime, however, the Auld Alliance seemed to have acquired a deeper reality. It was agreed that all citizens of both countries should automatically have dual nationality. In our time, enthusiastic Scottish francophiles who have studied the legalities insist that the right of dual nationality did not lapse until 1906, and that Scots born before then can still claim French citizenship.

The kingdom Mary had inherited was still no model of peace or prosperity. The Catholic-Protestant situation was becoming explosive. Mary's mother, Mary of Guise, acting as

Left: The young Queen Mary Stuart leaves Scotland for France in 1548. (From about this time the former usual spelling Stewart is often replaced by Stuart, the French form.)

Regent, was a devout Catholic. She had no particular hatred of Protestants but she knew the value of the Catholic clergy in keeping the Alliance firm, and would not have the Catholic church undermined or reformed.

The Queen Regent had no responsibility for the next horrifying martyrdom, when the new Bishop of St Andrews, Hamilton (who was Beaton's half-brother) had a man of eighty-two, Walter Myln, burned at the stake. His death, instead of driving the Protestants underground, raised a torrent of anger across the country and demand for reformation of the church. The Queen Regent in turn took a harder line, with the idea that if the rebellion got out of hand, she could get armed help from France. And later she did.

She was particularly offended to discover that on Easter Sunday of 1559, people in Dundee and Perth had simply not attended Mass. She blamed four preachers for the absence, and called them to account to her at Stirling. It looked like a dangerous encounter, for the clerics, and the lairds in the Dundee district met and decided that they would accompany the preachers. And suddenly John Knox was there too, his bondage in the galleys ended. He was part of the host that travelled to Perth, on the way to Stirling, and on 11 May 1559 gave a service in the parish church, and a fiery sermon condemning mass as idolatry.

Then there was one of those little incidents that keep history rolling. The incumbent priest was bent on celebrating Mass regardless, and when Knox was finished, he started moving to the altar. A boy in the congregation shouted at him, and the tight-lipped priest slapped him on the head. The boy retaliated by throwing a stone, which missed the priest and broke an image. He had suddenly invented a national sport. People all round looked for stones to throw at images, and smashed every one visible.

It was a game that would spread through the country, and escalate to the destruction of entire churches by what Knox called the rascall multitude. A by-product of the Reformation was to be the rejection of most that had been beautiful, or colourful, in the Catholic churches. In St Andrews, where the ruins of the cathedral are still an arresting sight, the very stonework was stolen for building cottages.

One notable survivor is Glasgow Cathedral, where the city's guild of stonemasons surrounded the building to hold back any of that destructive multitude. It became, and is still, the Protestant Cathedral in the city, and visitors may see, in the Necropolis behind it, a statue of John Knox on a tall pillar, apparently shaking his fist at it; or at the rascall multitude. But it was Knox's spellbinding oratory that roused the devil in his hearers, and launched open war between the Regent and the Protestants. Following the riot at Perth she set out

with an army to attack the Protestants at Cupar, but then decided against it. She retreated to Edinburgh and was driven out of the capital.

It was then that help came from France, and

Above: The martyrdom of Walter Myln, from a contemporary engraving.

the Queen Regent took control of Scotland again. It was then too that Henry II of France died, so that young Mary Stuart and her husband ascended the throne of France.

That Mary was also Queen of Scots was only one of the everyday complications. Another was that Catholics regarded Elizabeth of England, daughter of the heretic Henry VIII, as illegitimate, and considered Mary the rightful Queen of England too. And she thought they had the right idea, so she assumed the coats of arms of all three countries.

Things seemed fairly simple to the Scottish Protestant leaders, the Lords of the Congregation. The country was in the grip of France, the Lords did not have the muscle to expel them, and the only remedy, however desperate and dangerous, was to look for help from England. England was happy to give it, for whatever reasons, and dispatched a fleet and an army to Scotland in 1560 which forced the French into submission. They agreed to abandon Scotland under the Treaty of Edinburgh. In the same year the Scottish Parliament demonstrated the national hatred of compromise by not only repudiating the Pope, but by prohibiting the Mass altogether.

In the shifting ground of monarchical poli-

tics, there was another figure, Lord James Hamilton, kinsman of Queen Mary, who had the splendid idea that his son the Earl of Arran should marry Elizabeth of England and become head of both kingdoms. Elizabeth, as it turned out, was not the marrying kind. And suddenly Mary was back in Scotland, widowed before she was twenty, and the undoubted Queen of Scots.

A fundamental problem to her was that she was a Catholic, reigning over a country where the Mass was forbidden, and she did not mean to change her ways. Mass was celebrated in her Edinburgh palace of Holyrood, and there was an ugly incident when a mob of incensed Protestants tried to break in and murder the priest. But Mary did not interfere in the persecution of her fellow-Catholics by Protestant zealots. She also suffered, fairly courteously, the harangues which John Knox felt obliged, and happy, to throw at her. Having borne the galleys and the possibility of burning at the hands of an intolerant church, Knox, the great preacher, had a vision of a Scotland in which a new intolerance would pursue Catholicism to extinction.

He had other visions less brutal, of instituting free education for all classes, and this vision

Opposite, below: John Knox. After his time in the French galleys following his capture at St Andrews, Knox lived in England and then Switzerland before his return to Scotland in 1555. He left again soon after but came back finally in 1559.

Below: Knox preaching before the Lords of the Congregation, the Protestant leaders, in 1559, an engraving after the painting by Wilkie.

Left: The entry of Mary Queen of
Scots into Edinburgh in August
1561 after her return from France.

slowly took shape to give his country a
standard of universal education second to none
in Europe.

If Knox was a constant pain to the Queen,
there was another man who brought delight to
her heart, Henry Darnley. Tall, graceful, handsome, like Mary a Catholic, like Mary a descendant of Mary Tudor of England. She
married him in 1565, and in no time discovered
she had made a disastrous mistake. He was
vain, pompous and stupid; sullen because he
did not get a king's powers, given to drinking
and gaming with his sycophantic friends, and
probably not excessively masculine. The
Queen took comfort in the company and
conversation of David Rizzio, her secretary, a
man with a ready wit and musical talent.

Darnley was not the only one who resented
Rizzio's position as court favourite, and Darnley was among the gang in March 1566 who
broke into the Queen's apartments in Holyrood and stabbed him to death, ignoring the
tears and screams of Mary.

The nature of Mary Queen of Scots has
fascinated writers, of fact and fiction, down to
the present day; partly because her story is in
itself a tragedy with Greek inevitability, partly
because of her beauty, and partly because she
emerges as a puzzling blend of naivete, ruth-
lessness, cunning and stupidity. She certainly
had charm, and after the horrifying experience
of Rizzio's murder, she put her mind to
punishing the villains.

Darnley, she suspected, had been persuaded

into the outrage, he was never an initiator. And since she was still Queen, and to be feared, she set out to dazzle him, to win him over, to make a split in the ranks of the ungodly. She did it. She kept her feelings to herself. When the Protestant Lords led by the Earl of Moray proposed that she should formally issue a pardon to the murderers, she consented. It was not a situation any young woman would have envied. Moray himself had lately returned from England, where he had been hoping to recruit the help of Elizabeth in overthrowing the Scottish Queen. That help was refused not on principle, but because Elizabeth did not rate very highly his chances of success.

Superficially reconciled to her husband, Mary was certainly considering how she could get rid of him. She bore him a son, James, but that is because it was the duty of queens to bear sons to guarantee the succession. It was not from love, more from hate, that she permitted him his final useful act. Her heart, in a blend of romanticism and calculation, had turned to another of the nobles, the Earl of Bothwell, selfish and conceited, but a man in all the senses that Darnley was not. The idea of her marrying Bothwell was plainly insane. He was already married, apart from being a Protestant.

He might be able to escape from his marriage, but there was no possibility of Mary's divorcing Darnley. But there were many vigorous people in Scotland who had no love for Darnley either, Bothwell for one, and his co-conspirators, for his apparent defection back to the Queen's side. Another of those very Scottish cabals was formed, and had a meeting with the Queen. They proposed, and she approved, that Darnley should be removed. She approved on condition that whatever happened, and however it happened, her honour should be unsullied.

Above: Henry Stewart, Lord Darnley, 1545-67, married Mary Queen of Scots in July 1565. Darnley was descended from James II of Scotland and from Margaret Tudor, widow of James IV, and so he had a claim to both the Scots and the English thrones but despite his dynastic suitability he proved a poor match for Mary.

Left: The Murder of Rizzio by Sir William Allan. The horrified pregnant queen looks on as her favourite is stabbed.

Left: Mary Queen of Scots and her husband Henry Lord Darnley.

Royal honour is often a matter of practical politics. In 1567, Darnley was in Glasgow, ill probably with smallpox. Mary travelled there and cajoled him into coming with her to Edinburgh. In hindsight, it could be seen that the journey was tidily planned ahead. They stopped outside Edinburgh to stay in Kirk o' Field, an old monastery, where she was pleasant and sociable for several days, until she remembered that she had promised to attend the wedding of a maid of honour, and left for Holyrood. It was around the anniversary of the murder of Rizzio.

Soon after her departure, an immense explosion completely destroyed Kirk o' Field. Current belief was that Darnley had died in the explosion, and probably that was what the killers had intended. Modern investigation, guided by professional knowledge of explosives, shows that it was a botched job of simulation. There was no chance that the gunpowder could have guaranteed the death, and Darnley had in fact been garrotted and left to vanish in the explosion. Instead, he was found dead but without a mark of burning.

Bothwell was the prime suspect in the killing. There were graffiti in Edinburgh accusing him of it. He kept his nerve. Darnley's father the Earl of Lennox demanded that he should be arraigned for murder, and the Queen made a show of doing this, but on the day when he might have been tried, Bothwell was in Edinburgh with a small army of determined gangsters of his own, and Lennox was afraid to come to the capital. It blew over, for the moment.

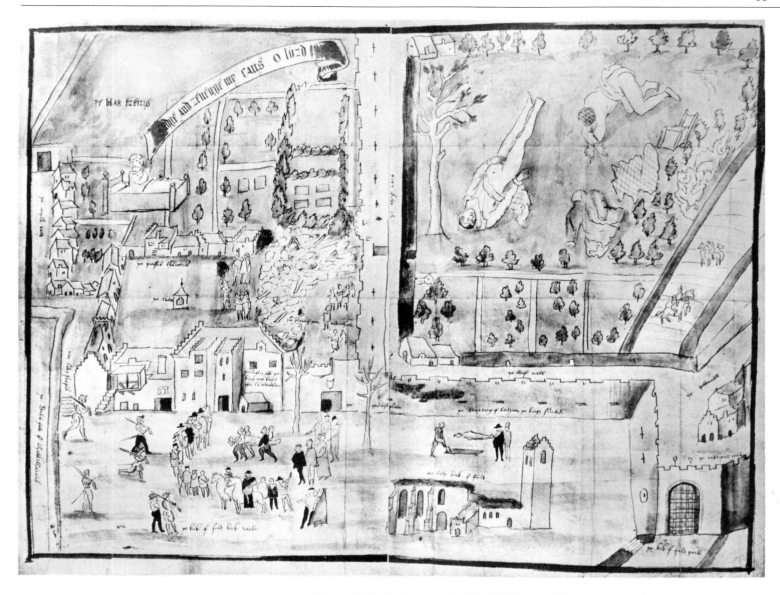

It was obvious that whatever other motives she might have, however much she might be concerned with the health and the future of Scotland, Mary was besotted with Bothwell. There was an absurd piece of play-acting when the Queen, on her way from a visit to her child in Stirling, was halted before she could reach Edinburgh, by a group of armed men headed by Bothwell, and taken instead to Dunbar Castle. He did not need armed men. The Queen was his.

Politically, her plan, or her unplanned determination, was crazy. Bothwell was organising a sort of shotgun divorce to free himself for great things, but marriage between these two was likely to undermine the throne completely. Bothwell, on the other hand, had nothing to lose, and marriage it was. A bare three months after the death of Darnley, he was married to the Queen in Holyrood, in a hole-in-the-corner ceremony attended by a few cynical nobles.

The union was a national scandal, and rebellion was automatic. The loving couple escaped to Dunbar, raised some kind of force and made for Edinburgh again, to be halted by a superior group of rebels who said that they had no fight

Above: A contemporary sketch of the murder of Darnley at Kirk o' Field. Darnley's body appears at top right while at top left his infant son (James VI) prays for revenge.

Left: Mary Queen of Scots and her young son, the future James VI and I.

Left: Miniature portraits of Bothwell and his first wife, Lady Jean Gordon, believed to date from 1566. Bothwell divorced her in the hope of marrying Queen Mary.

with the Queen, but only with the treacherous murderer of her husband. The Queen parleyed with them while Bothwell slipped away to Dunbar, where he caught a ship to Norway just ahead of the rebels in chase. He died in exile.

Mary had no such luck. She was carried to Edinburgh where the fickle crowds jeered and cursed. She was forced to abdicate the throne in favour of the infant James; the Earl of Moray became Regent, and she was imprisoned in the island castle of Loch Leven. The golden dream had faded.

She did not give up. She spent a year in Loch Leven, incommunicado, but there was

always some group who could see advantage in undermining the other group, and this time it was the Hamilton's, who reckoned that if they could secure possession of the Queen, they could marry her to Lord Claude. If that seems impractical, in view of the fact that she was already married to the absent Bothwell, it was the kind of detail that rarely inhibited dynastic enthusiasts.

And at least their organisation of the Queen's escape was miraculously practical, and ingenious. The gates of Loch Leven Castle were locked every evening. But the Queen was free to stroll on the island during the day, and

Below: Queen Mary is brought to Edinburgh as a prisoner after the defeat of Mary's and Bothwell's forces at Carberry Hill in 1567. In fact there was little fighting before Bothwell fled and the queen's army dispersed.

Left: The ruined cathedral at St Andrews.

Below: Loch Leven Castle, scene of Queen Mary's imprisonment in 1567-8.

however it was organised, one evening when the gates were locked, she was not in the castle.

The guards heard a boat being rowed in the darkness towards the loch shore, and found that the rowlocks of all the other boats had vanished. Mary was home and dry, with a party of horsemen to meet her on the far shore and take her to Hamilton. Her own plan was to escape to France, which would involve getting to Dumbarton in the west to board ship. To stop her, the Regent put an army into Glasgow.

The two forces clashed at Langside, to the south of Glasgow, and after a brief battle the Queen saw that it was hopeless, and fled south. Her last resort was to seek haven with her kinswoman Elizabeth in London. It was not a haven. To Elizabeth, Mary was the prime threat to her own tenure of the English throne, the blood lines of the two women were interlaced in such complexity. The cousinly hospitality Mary might have expected was instead imprisonment; an imprisonment that was to last almost twenty hopeless years until Elizabeth herself wearied of it. Documents, virtually certainly forged, were produced to convict Mary of conspiracy to murder Queen Elizabeth, and in 1587 the Queen of Scots knelt to put her head on the block, asking the headsman to strike straight and true.

Right: James Stewart, Earl of Moray, 1531-1570, illegitimate son of James V and Regent during James VI's minority until assassinated in 1570.

Below: A somewhat fanciful Victorian view of the assassination of Moray. In fact Moray was shot from a staircase window as he and a group of his men rode in the street in Linlithgow.

It was hardly surprising that Elizabeth should get rid of her awkward kinswoman, Mary. It was sad that the deed was done almost with the complicity of Mary's son, James. By the time of the execution he had ascended the Scottish throne, and he was advised in advance by Elizabeth. A shrewd politician, James VI protested publicly, but made it clear privately to the English queen that his protests would not take any practical form. Two years earlier, in fact, he had agreed a treaty with the English, and he had no intention of breaking it.

Possibly James had grown up with a liking for quick simple solutions, because during his time as a boy king, the old Scottish schisms went on and on. The Earl of Moray as Regent knew that there would be no peace in his time. He was beset by intrigue on several sides, and two factions started to spring up in the land: the King's Lords and the Queen's Lords. As always, both loyalties and moralities were confused. The King's Lords were determined, among other things, to maintain the Protestant faith in Scotland. They were also determined to get their share of wealth and power, of course.

The Queen's Lords were not necessarily in favour of the Catholic church, simply in favour of the Queen. Believing that her passion for Bothwell must have faded away, they could see no reason why she should not resume the throne. Elizabeth, of course, did not agree, and Elizabeth held that particular card. But the war went on, a squalid affair that started when Hamilton assassinated the Regent in 1570.

The new regent was the boy-king's grandfather, Lennox, whose appointment was favoured by Elizabeth. The trouble went on. The Queen's Lords took possession of Edinburgh Castle and controlled the town. Lennox and the King's Lords set up their Parliament in Stirling. The country had two Parliaments and very little in the way of law and order from either of them.

The Edinburgh set, in fact, conducted a night raid on Stirling and took prisoner the Regent and the entire body of the King's Lords. Before they could be shipped to Edinburgh, the people of Stirling intervened, and the raiders were chased out of town. Regent Lennox, however, was among the dead.

The new Regent was the Earl of Mar, who was no more successful than Lennox in uniting the battered country. What he wanted was military aid from England to storm Edinburgh Castle and be rid of the rebels, but Elizabeth put him off. He died after only a few months in power and was replaced by the Earl of Morton. It was less Morton's strength than the climate of the time that started to erode the position of the Queen's Lords. Their cause was hopeless and they grew tired of it. And finally came the English artillery that the Regent had been waiting for, and the Edinburgh Castle garrison was battered into surrender.

Morton set himself to govern Scotland with ruthless efficiency. He made enemies, but he was equal to them, until a new one arrived on the scene from France. This was a very smooth individual, Esmé Stuart, related (like so many

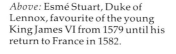

Above: Esmé Stuart, Duke of Lennox, favourite of the young King James VI from 1579 until his return to France in 1582.

Left: James Douglas, 4th Earl of Morton, Regent from 1572-79, was the last of the Douglas family to act at the centre of Scottish affairs.

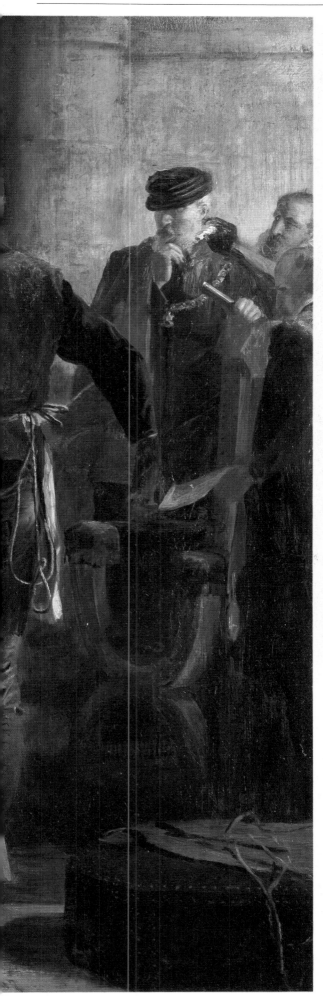

Above: Mary Queen of Scots. (The Morton or Dalmahoy portrait by an unknown artist.)

people) to the King, and so ingratiating that the King appointed him Lord High Chamberlain and gave him the Lennox title.

Stuart was, of course, a Catholic, and it may be that he had in mind a return for Scotland to the Roman Church. His method of dealing with Morton was crude and abrupt. One of his hangers-on accused Morton of having been involved in the killing of Darnley. The charge was found proven and Morton executed. Lennox was master.

The King's own position in all this is ambiguous. His relationship with the Frenchman does suggest that he was toying with a return to Catholicism, although the Frenchman himself had publicly disavowed the Roman faith. Three Scottish nobles, Mar, Gowrie and Glencairn, were deeply suspicious of the relationship and of Stuart's intentions, and they kidnapped the King and took over power.

Left: Execution of Mary, Queen of Scots by Robert Herdman.

IACOBVS · 6 · D · G · R
SCOTORVM
ÆTA · 29 ·
1595 ·

Esmé Stuart left for France, and never returned to Scotland.

The King escaped, and next turned to another Stuart, the Earl of Arran, for advice and counsel. He too saw dangerous times ahead for him and left the country. The truth probably is that the King was simply biding his time and hedging his bets and waiting to see what course, what policy, would be best for himself. He was certainly very friendly to many of the Catholic nobles, even when they were managing minor rebellions. But he was still young, Elizabeth was getting older, and the throne of England still was the glittering prize.

It was not automatically to fall to James. The Virgin Queen had no heir, would have no heir, but although she was happy to sign treaties with James, she would not discuss the succession. Still, her throne would certainly never go to a Catholic; and James was a shrewd even cunning man who wanted everything. Not physically heroic, but very resolute and capable of guile to get his way.

He spent his time as King of Scots partly in trying at last to enforce some kind of law on the land, in reorganising Parliament and making it work better. He held to the firm Stuart doctrine of the Divine Right of Kings, because he simply believed that it was ordained by God and that divine policy was the best policy. It was a belief that was to bring its own trouble to the Stuart dynasty in time.

Now, the Stuart dynasty was in the ascendant. On Saturday 27 March 1603, a weary

Left: George Buchanan, scholar and historian, was tutor to the young King James and gave his charge a gruelling but thorough education.

messenger from London arrived late at night at the Palace of Holyrood, and said that he must see the King, though James was already in bed. Taken to the King, he acclaimed him King of England, Scotland, France and Ireland. The inclusion of France is simply explained by the determination of monarchs never to give up even the most tenuous title to any throne at all.

And so Scotland and her Auld Enemy were one, or at least under one king. It was peace at last.

Opposite: James VI, as he appeared in 1595, in a painting attributed to Adrian Vanson.

Left: The so-called Gowrie conspiracy of 1600 may have been a plot to assassinate King James but since the alleged assassins were quickly killed there remains some doubt as to the accuracy of the official account.

TO PROCLAIM peace at last in a Scottish context is asking for trouble and rebuttal. It did seem, indeed, that the country was settling down on the accession of its king to the throne of England. Turbulence was of course to come.

When we ask the question, Nation or Province? we do it in hindsight. The ordinary Scot did not feel in any way diminished, or pushed out from the centre of things by the Union of the Crowns. He was probably proud and pleased that a Scot was ruling England as well as Scotland.

And James certainly felt that he was ruling Scotland, although it was now far away – ruling it with no effort whatever, where so many previous monarchs had tried hard and failed. And he did rule it from a distance. After his arrival in London, he visited Scotland only once during the rest of his life.

In hindsight, certainly, many Scots have complained that he moved his court to London at all. Being the established head of both nations, he might well have exercised his privilege by making Edinburgh the centre of the United Kingdom. His desertion, as they see it, had effects on the Scottish psyche which have persisted into modern times.

His reasons for settling in the South are quite plain, of course. Scotland in his time, and for a long time afterwards, was by no means a heaven in the material sense. Life by our standards, even for the wealthy, was a crude and certainly insanitary affair, the diet was boring, the houses were cold and draughty, epidemics were routine – nobody connected them at the time with putrefaction. London was a much more cosy and luxurious ambience for anyone entitled (as all the Stuarts were, of course) to expect the best.

One of the effects of the king's translation, at any rate, was to accentuate as time went by the Scot's sense of distance from the heart of the country, from the decision-making centre, from the big-time operation of the body politic; and at the same time strengthen the London consciousness of being that nerve-centre, innately superior to the far-flung provinces.

And wherever the court went, the courtiers went. Over the following century, Scotland's nobles were largely in Scotland, some of them from time to time waging war on one another. But the pull of the south was very strong. The sons of the mighty began to acquire the education, and the manners, and the speech of the metropolitan upper classes, and it would be a rare and startling experience today to find a member of a Scottish noble family who does not speak in a southern English accent.

This is not too trivial. The way we speak is an important part of who we are. And King James, at least formally, presided over a superb creation which intensified, in time, the Scottish

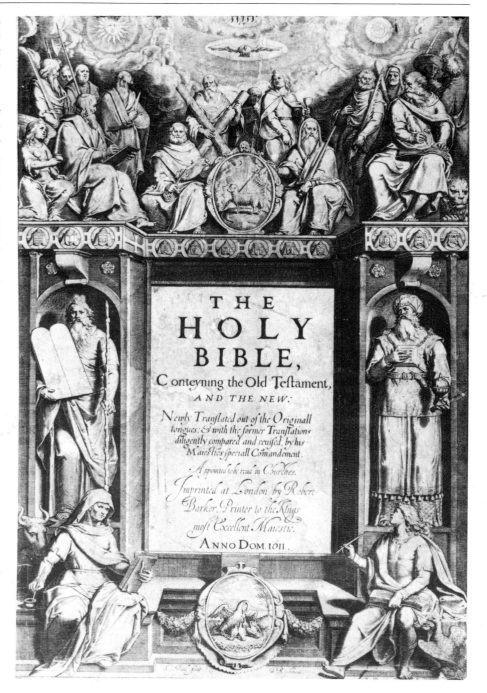

feeling of remoteness: the Authorised Version of the Bible.

The translation of Scripture into the 'vernacular' was a logical process in the rejection of Papal authority both in England and in Scotland. And it was done, in England, in a period when the English language – the English language of southern England, that is – was in its magnificent flower. Shakespeare was only the towering peak of that golden age, there were also Marlowe and Johnson and Bacon, a king might write a sonnet, and the language had a majesty that still rings. That was the age in which the Bible came into English.

Translations into other European languages are not generally regarded as anything but translations. They are not hailed as great literature. The English Bible certainly is. And here, suddenly, was another confusion for the

Above: The title page from an early edition of the Authorised or King James' Version of the Bible.

Previous page: Bonnie Prince Charlie leaving Scotland as seen in the painting *Lochaber No More* by J B MacDonald.

literate Scot. He spoke English, but his own (perfectly legitimate) form of English, which we now call Scots. He was also, of course, passionately religious and even theological.

With the new Bible in his hand, he discovered that while he talked about the mundane things of life, farming, working, eating, feeling, in his own language, Scots, God spoke English. Among many Scots, especially Scots of limited education in the history of language, this conviction has produced a feeling of inferiority.

That was a little in the future. What was firm fact as James exercised his power over his homeland, was that the Reformation, the proud Scottish assertion of its own religious rights, and rites, was not as secure as it had seemed. James had reinstated the bishops in the year before his English accession. When he did revisit Scotland in 1617, for the only time, he had an organ installed in the Holyrood chapel, and enjoyed a totally Episcopal service. In 1618 he bludgeoned the General Assembly of the Scottish church into accepting increased power for bishops, making worship compulsory on Christmas Day, Easter Day, and other days venerated by the English church, supposedly without specific scriptural authority.

He also, by the exercise of a little underhanded diplomacy, effectively controlled the composition of the Scottish Parliament. James

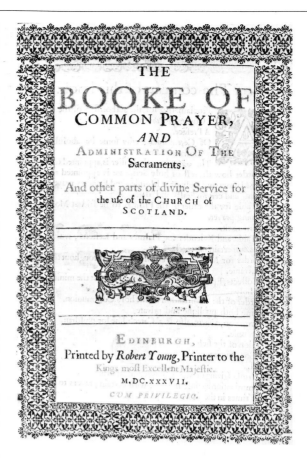

Left: An edition of the Book of Common Prayer dating from 1637. There was widespread resistance to Charles I's attempts to impose what were seen as Episcopalian forms on the church in Scotland.

Below: Jenny Geddes provokes a riot in St Giles in Edinburgh in 1637 in protest against the use of the new forms of church service. Although this is commonly portrayed as a spontaneous outbreak of popular indignation there is evidence that the incident was carefully planned and contrived.

was a Stuart through and through. He knew that the king knew best, and that the king must

instrumental music in church was feared as the work of the devil. Singing of praise was led by a precentor. He would sing each line solo and the congregation would repeat it.

The most important part of a church service was the sermon, which could last for a very long time, but had to be endured if it was not enjoyed. In one way, this Presbyterianism was a rejection of anything gentle or joyful. It had not merely expunged the evidences of Romanism, the colour, the ornamentation, the choir, but had crushed other, non-religious entertainments. In earlier times, the Scots had enjoyed little celebrations of absurdity, like harmless Saturnalia, with rituals like those of the Abbot of Misrule, or Robin Hood and midsummer night bonfires. Even the Catholic church condemned these as pagan. The Presbyterian church made the portrayal of Robin Hood a capital crime.

One citizen who proposed to lead this harmless romp in Edinburgh was seized, and his friends appealed to the Provost and John Knox, who deliberated as conscientious Christians and confirmed the death sentence. His friends rescued him; but the climate was against jollity, and continued that way into the seventeenth century. Theatre, flourishing magically in London, did not exist in Scotland, and could not exist.

This almost barbaric austerity undoubtedly gave the Scots a sense of utter conviction and rectitude, and the unyielding moral courage to resist to the death any king or prelate who tried to dilute the pure gospel. And when James's son Charles succeeded to the throne in 1625, they had even more to resist. Charles had no acquaintance with Scotland, which he had left as a child. His own Episcopal faith was so rigid and formalised as to be very close to Catholicism, and he too believed he knew what was best for the common people.

When he visited Scotland in 1633 to be crowned, he had an Anglican service in St Giles in Edinburgh, which was promoted to the level of cathedral. And he ordained that the Scottish churches should shed their austerity and be decorated and furnished as in England. There would also be, he ordered, no spontaneous prayers, but only proven recitals from the Book of Common Prayer. The Scots saw this, naturally, as the thin edge of the Roman wedge. When preachers in St Giles dared to intone from the Episcopal book, worshippers howled them down – particularly female worshippers. One of them, Jenny Geddes, earned a small corner in history for throwing her stool at the preacher and shouting 'You daurna say Mass at my lug!' ('Don't dare say Mass in my ear!')

The Scots enthusiasts found what looked like a way of being loyal and unyielding at the same time, in the shape of the National Covenant of 1638, which affirmed their loyalty but rejected the idea of any customs being imposed on the

Above: King James VI of Scotland and I of England painted by an unknown artist in 1618. Although James only came to Scotland once after his accession to the English throne his knowledge of Scottish affairs and of the leading families in Scotland helped him govern his original kingdom more ably than his son and successor Charles I who had no such background.

impose that best on his people, who did not share his divine understanding. He never abandoned his efforts to restore Episcopacy, both in form and in content.

The attitude of the Scots, as always, was ambivalent. They accepted the king but they stuck to their own revelations. And the Presbyterianism they practised was a hard unyielding faith. In some ways it was closer to Judaism than to Christianity as other sects understood it. It was deeply suspicious of Christmas, and abominated graven images such as the crucifix. It did not recognise Easter as a celebration.

It was also deeply suspicious of anything soft or beautiful. Paintings in the old churches had usually been painted over, stained glass windows were replaced with plain glass, and church except those decided by a free General Assembly of the church. Great queues lined up to sign it, copies were sent all over the country, and it amounted to a national referendum, and indeed, a declaration of war.

Charles found this very inconvenient. He had nothing in the shape of an army, and very little money to equip one, because the English Parliament was unexpectedly independent about giving him money for anything he desired. He did manage to raise a force of some kind in 1639 and send it into Scotland, but the stubborn Scots army, under Alexander Leslie, were waiting for it, clearly superior in force, and there was a reluctant peace.

Scotland's Parliament was flexing its muscles, and in the following year it probably abandoned any Episcopal tendencies and took over the power to legislate, displacing the king's puppet Privy Councillors. Leslie, foreseeing another attack from the king, took the initiative, marched his army over the border and took over the north of England. The king was forced, bitterly, to yield again, and after a long process of haggling accepted a treaty which gave Scotland and its Parliament their rights.

Charles did not really have the pulse of the English Parliament, or the English people, any more than he was sensitive to the Scots, and in 1642 he had the Civil War on his hands.

The Scots viewed this affair over the Border very warily. Oliver Cromwell soon came to lead the English Parliamentarians and though a

Below: The signing of the National Covenant in Greyfriars Churchyard in Edinburgh in 1638.

anism; and at the battle of Marston Moor in 1644, another Leslie, the talented David Leslie, and his men had quite as large a part to play in downing the Royalists as had Cromwell's famous Ironsides.

Unfortunately, a rebellion arose in Scotland, a royalist rebellion under Montrose who led an army raised in the Highlands and brilliantly conquered much of the country. His was a barren victory which was swept away when David Leslie came north to the Borders and routed Montrose's depleted force. Montrose himself escaped, with some of his followers. Those who did not were slaughtered by Leslie's good Presbyterians, down to women camp followers and their children.

Charles had another try at rousing the Scots to humiliate his rebellious English subjects, when he visited Scotland in 1646, but absolutely refused to agree to the establishment of Presbyterianism. In a way, he and the Scots deserved each other. Each side was totally, and blindly, besotted with its own principles, to the death and beyond, and incapable of admitting even a small error. There was a minor skirmish against the English Parliament by a party under the Duke of Hamilton, but the raid was a fiasco and Hamilton was executed. This did not stop Cromwell from being given a hero's welcome when he visited Edinburgh in 1649.

The execution of the king a little later turned

stern Puritan seemed rather over-tolerant of other religions to many Scots. Nonetheless they finally decided to support the Parliamentary side against the king in the quite inane belief that they would be rewarded by the imposition of compulsory Presbyteri-

Left: James Graham, Marquis of Montrose had been a leading supporter of the National Covenant but went over to the king's side when other supporters of the Covenant adopted more extreme policies. Montrose proved to be an excellent general but was unable to hold together his army of Highlanders for an extended campaign.

Below: The defeat of Montrose at Philiphaugh in September 1645. Most of Montrose's army had returned to Ireland or the Highlands and the remains were defeated by David Leslie's Covenanters.

the country against Cromwell, and towards accepting Charles II as King of Scotland, since the new king did agree to sign the Covenant. Cromwell invaded, and now David Leslie, who had fought so well at his side, was his enemy. The Scots were defeated at a final battle near Dunbar, but they were not convinced of it, and did have Charles II crowned at Scone. A couple of years later Cromwell returned in greater strength and finally crushed the rebellion.

The country which had started this chapter with its king as the supreme lord of a united Britain was now a conquered country living under an army of occupation. The regime was not too harsh, but Cromwell was bored with the pestilential Scots. He put his own puppets into the Scottish Parliament, took it over and merged it with the English. The thirty representatives from Edinburgh who went to Westminster to speak for Scotland were almost all English.

The Restoration of the Monarchy in 1660 was something in which Scotland had no hand, but it was welcomed with relief in the land. The relief was, predictably, unjustified. The endless business of bishops or no bishops was a live issue again. The revived Scottish Parliament was a feeble affair, well under the king's thumb, and Charles had no interest in a Covenant which had been convenient when he signed it but was now just a nuisance. He had the bishops reinstalled, and the bishops alone had the power to appoint parish ministers. Some ministers, some worshippers, gave in for the sake of peace. Others rejected the churches and became the Covenanters, going into the hills to worship privately in the open air at services known as conventicles. Failure to attend church was now punishable by fines, and when one aggressive group showed fight, it was attacked by dragoons. Thirty of the worshippers were hanged and the rest sent to slavery. This merely turned the Covenant into a secret army, armed for defence and ready to fight.

For year after year the authorities tried to extirpate the secret worship. For year after year the Covenanters fought back. One preacher, Richard Cameron, declared open rebellion with a handful of parishioners. All were killed.

The situation worsened with the death of Charles II and the accession of his Catholic

Above: A cartoon from 1651 showing Charles II being lectured to by his Scots subjects. Despite the defeat at Dunbar a Scots army went with Charles to the final decisive defeat at Worcester.

brother, James VII. Under his rule, attending a Covenanting act of worship was a capital crime, and many Presbyterians paid the penalty. In typical Stuart fashion, of course, James alienated all the people whose support he depended on, and he was ousted from the throne in 1688, the last of his line to wear a crown.

He had been ousted, at the request of the English Parliament, by William of Orange. But while he accepted his exile, others did not. One was Graham of Claverhouse Viscount Dundee, who decided to raise an army of liberation. He went quietly through the Highlands, gathering willing clansmen for war.

When the news filtered south, General Mackay was dispatched to crush the rebellion. His army's route lay through the Pass of Killiecrankie where it was particularly vulnerable to attack. They negotiated the Pass without incident, but at the head of the Pass were the troops of Bonnie Dundee.

The regular troops followed their routine of firing a musket volley and then fixing bayonets to charge. They had no time to fix the bayonets before the wild Highlanders were on them, screaming and flailing their claymores. Mackay's men were killed in hundreds. The

Left: A monument to martyred Covenanters at Hamilton.

Opposite: Condemned Covenanters being taken for execution in Edinburgh. The period of the greatest oppression of the Covenanters, the 1680s, has become known as the 'killing time' but this term exaggerates the degree and extent of the troubles. Many more Scots probably died during the 1690s when there was a succession of bad harvests.

Below: The Covenanters' Preaching by Sir George Harvey gives a comfortable Victorian view of what must have been a far less tranquil scene in reality.

general was one of the survivors who were able to flee.

It was total victory for Dundee, but he himself was killed in the clash, and the Highlanders were leaderless. They did keep together for an attack on Dunkeld, which was garrisoned by Cameronians (as the Covenanters had become known), at least as fierce and better disciplined than the rebels. Outnumbered four to one, the Cameronians held out till they wore out their attackers, and the Highlanders finally abandoned the assault, and the war of liberation, and drifted back to their native glens.

Scotland did not quite settle down to peaceful times. There were old divisions too precious to be discarded. Loyal or not to William, they had a bitter sense of grievance against him. They had objected to the intolerance, the anti-Presbyterian intolerance, of the Stuarts. They were almost equally outraged by the tolerance of William.

William has a curious place in Scottish legend as the valiant champion of the Protestant cause against the Catholic. It is true he did rid Britain of a Catholic king; but to him it was a political and not a religious operation. He had no animus against Catholics, had friendly relations with the Pope, had been generous to monasteries in his time, and had Catholics in the army he led to victory at the Battle of the Boyne in Northern Ireland. The fact that he has been adopted as a kind of patron saint of hardline Protestantism by later generations is irrelevant to the history of his own time.

The Scots Presbyterians evidently felt that they had a champion in William, a king who would conscript everybody into the Presbyterian church, willy-nilly. Instead William took the eccentric view that if it had been wrong for Episcopalians to persecute the Presbyterians, it was equally wrong for the persecution to be operated in reverse. There were to be no witch-hunts. Many former Episcopalians left the church, which became, in effect, the Church of Scotland more or less as it exists in our time (though, naturally, there have been numerous internal disputes, schisms and breakaways. It is, after all, a Scottish church.) But in spite of the passionate pleas of enthusiastic Presbyterians who wanted God's will done at once on earth, the Piskies were not prosecuted, not exiled, not massacred.

The constitution of the Church rejected the idea of the monarch as religious head. It was to be, and is, an utterly democratic institution, in which every worshipper has direct contact with God, and the minister is elected by the congregation, as its servant. The General Assembly, which in truth has been a sort of Scottish Parliament, though without legislative powers, is an annual gathering of clergy and laymen, and its chairman, the Moderator, is a parish minister who holds office for only a year before returning to his parish duties. All men,

and women, in the theology of the Church of Scotland, are equal in the sight of God.

After all the strife, the bloody toil, the rival persecutions, the purblind prejudices and the fraternal hatreds, the Scots produced a form of religion which is possibly as close to the original message of Christ as any nation has come; that belief is of course open to dispute.

With religious peace came the need for political peace, particularly among the Highlanders, who were largely cut off from Lowland society, and who included many still loyal to the deposed King James.

William, very simply, was not very interested in Scotland. His principal minister for Scotland was the lairdling John Dalrymple, the Master of Stair, who took charge of the royal ordinance that every chief of the Highland clans must abandon that old Stuart loyalty and swear fealty to William. There was a closing date: New Year's Day, 1692. And there was to be a legendary bloodbath as a consequence of that ordinance.

The clan chiefs did what was asked. One minor chieftain MacIan of the Clan Mac-Donald, got it wrong. He took his oath to Fort

Above: General Tam Dalyell (an ancestor of the present-day Member of Parliament of the same name) was the commander-in-chief of the royal forces in Scotland 1666-85. Dalyell won an important early victory over the Covenanters at Rullion Green in 1666. The painting is by Schuneman.

Right: The Battle of Drumclog, 1679, a victory for the Covenanters over the government forces led by Graham of Claverhouse.

Top, far right: James Graham of Claverhouse, Viscount Dundee, is now remembered for the rising he led in favour of the deposed James VII and II until his death at Killiecrankie. (Painting from the studio of Sir Peter Lely).

William in good time, but was told that the proper place was Inveraray. In the deep midwinter, he got to Inveraray days late, but in fact earlier than the Sheriff who was to accept his declaration. The Sheriff accepted the oath.

No matter. The Master of Stair had some personal hatred of the MacDonalds, took the legalistic view that the late declaration was invalid, and ordered a Campbell Chieftain, Campbell of Glenlyon, to extirpate the MacDonalds he detested.

The scene was the valley of Glencoe, which to this day has a bleak and forbidding atmosphere even in the brightest sunshine, as if the hills remembered the black treachery and the blood.

Glencoe is where the little community of MacDonalds lived. In February, they were visited by the Campbells, and received them hospitably – the chieftains were related through marriage. Campbell and his armed troops stayed for two weeks and made friends with their hosts, there was a lot of sociable drinking, but in the early morning of 13 February 1692 the guests arose and set about murdering their hosts. Women and children were not spared. Campbell's orders from Stair were to execute every MacDonald under the age of seventy.

In a sudden snowstorm, many of the MacDonalds escaped. Probably a couple of dozen, including the chieftain and his family, perished. It is not the scale, but the manner of

it, and the treachery of it, that has made Glencoe a fearful word, and given every Campbell a burden of accusation to bear, though the Campbells of Glenlyon were only one of a large number of Campbell communities – often at odds with one another –and were merely the tools of a callous politician.

The Scots cherish their tales of injustice, treachery and slaughter. People are still writing songs about the Massacre.

In the Lowlands, the Scots had quickly forgotten the claims of the ousted Stuarts, and accepted William as sovereign. But although Scots and English had one king, they did not

Above: Robert Campbell of Glenlyon who commanded the Massacre of Glencoe. The painting by an unknown artist shows Campbell as a young man; at the time of the massacre he was an embittered bankrupt in his sixties.

have equality. There are no ballads about Scotland's commercial expedition to the Darien peninsula; but compared with the score or so of victims in Glencoe, Darien claimed over two thousand dead.

Already, England, the senior partner in the alliance, was growing rich in far-flung trade, through such organisations as the African Company and the East India Company, and Scotland was rigorously excluded from any share in this growing wealth. William Paterson, the hyperactive entrepreneur who was later to found the Bank of England and invent the principle of the National Debt, saw colonial trading wealth for Scotland in Central America, in Darien.

King William did not approve. King William was really bored with the Scots.

Paterson's plan pre-dated the Panama Canal. He saw the isthmus as a place where goods destined for the far east could be landed, carried overland and transported across the Pacific. He had seen the area in the wrong season. In its own season it was a deathtrap of fever. And the Spaniards, who regarded Central America as their property, did not approve either. Military attacks helped disease to wipe out that Paterson dream. The colony got no help from the English possessions in the West Indies which did nothing to improve feelings between Scotland and England especially since most of the finance for the expedition had been raised by public subscription in Scotland.

The answer to all this should be the real union of the two countries, with one Parlia-

Left: The forbidding aspect of Glencoe.

ment. Both were darkly suspicious. England had her trade monopolies, her quiet assurance of superiority, her place at the centre of the world. Scotland had her pride, so often scarred. The Darien disaster had exposed the great divide between the two nations, and King William was now sure that a total union must be the answer.

It was not going to be a walkover. Here we may look at one individual Scot who was determined to make it difficult. Andrew Fletcher of Saltoun was a laird in Haddington, a man of electric wit and intellect at a time when these qualities were fairly scarce. He had been fiercely opposed to what he considered the autocratic rule of Charles II, and left Scotland for Europe in 1681 to be away from it. His

Below: Massacre of Glencoe by James Hamilton. As the painting suggests the massacre was incompetently carried out with many of the potential victims escaping from their homes. Despite the reputation the event has retained, contemporaries seem to have viewed it less seriously, for the MacDonalds of Glencoe and the Campbells of Glenlyon fought together during the 1715 Jacobite Rebellion.

departure was encouraged by his being out-
lawed and sentenced to death in his absence,
for his support of Monmouth's rebellion in
England.

All was forgiven and forgotten after the
overthrow of the Stuart monarchy. Fletcher
returned to Scotland, and became a vigorous
parliamentarian. He was seething with active
ideas, like a permanent militia, the introduction of slavery as a cure for vagrancy and
pauperism, and a Free Trade treaty with England, not a union. He proposed free trade as a

condition of Scotland's accepting Queen Anne as monarch of Scotland when William died in 1702.

Fletcher was one of those Scots who was happy to be in a minority and would probably have felt uneasy if everybody had agreed with him. When the question of Union arose in Parliament, he was passionately in favour of a federal union, not an absorption into England. That passion has never entirely died away in Scotland, and may rise again.

The very prospect of a union of parliaments provoked something very near to war between the two countries. The Scottish Parliament, with its Act of Security, reserved the right to accept or reject a monarch chosen by England. The English Parliament, with its Aliens Act, barred Scottish exports to England. English ships attacked and captured Scottish ships engaged in international trade.

In the end, the Treaty of Union of 1707 decreed the incorporation of the Scottish Parliament into the Westminster Parliament. There was a payment from England to Scotland of nearly £400,000, ostensibly to compensate for the losses of the Darien scheme. To many Scots it was simply a bribe to parliamentarians to give up their country's independence. That is how it was seen by Fletcher of Saltoun.

The last meeting of Parliament in Edinburgh was a formal, almost bleak affair. On 25 March 1707, it was finished. In the words of James Ogilvie, Lord Chancellor of Scotland, now there was the end of 'ane auld sang.'

But the melody did linger on, in the form of those persistent Stuarts. The son of James VII & II, who had never held the throne, nevertheless styled himself James VIII & III, and fretted for the reality of kingship. By 1714, the crown was worn by George I, a German. Romantic Scots would still drink the royal toast, but wave their glasses over the water jug to indicate that they meant the king in exile – across the water.

And Fletcher's forebodings about the Union were justified by, among other things, a punitive tax placed on Scottish malt by the united Parliament. The Earl of Marchmont, enraged, moved for the repeal of the Act of Union in the House of Lords. The majority against was only four. Clearly, the spirit of rebellion had not died out.

Louis XIV of France had proclaimed his support for James. Plans were made for the Pretender, as he was known, to sail to Scotland with a French force, recruit his supporters and march on England to restore the Stuart monarchy. Such a plan had petered out before, in 1708, when a French fleet had carried James to Fife, but at the sight of British warships, had turned tail without landing him.

It is doubtful if there was a big potential force ready to follow James among the Lowlanders. Many of the rural gentry were keen Jacobites, in theory. The ordinary Lowlanders had their

doubts. There was more hope for James in the Highlands, where the old loyalty still flourished.

The Earl of Mar was the man James chose to organise his crusade, and wrote to him asking for his help. Then he decided the time was not ripe (King Louis of France had died), wrote again telling Mar to call off the rising. But Mar had already acted, had rallied a group of lairds and chieftains to bring their men to Braemar.

The signs were favourable. There was support, at least verbal support, all over the North of Scotland, Mar occupied Perth and prepared to move south. But he delayed in Perth to await more recruits from the Highlands.

In the meantime, other Jacobite leaders in the Borders, both in Scotland and in England, had started to gather forces to join in, and Mar sent two thousand men to join them while he stayed in Perth. The expedition was blocked by regular forces near Stirling, and the Jacobite commander, Mackintosh of Borlum, diverted to take his men across the Firth of Forth in stolen fishing boats and march on Edinburgh. But after a skirmish there with the regular army

Above: James VIII and III, the Old Pretender, proved to be an uninspiring leader when he came to Scotland to lead the rebellion in 1715.

under the Duke of Argyll, he and his men made for the Borders, where they joined their allies and travelled south. They had no difficulty in taking Preston, but when a superior force of regulars mounted an attack, the Jacobites surrendered.

Mar's Highland reinforcements had meanwhile arrived at Perth and it was time for the invasion. His troops came face to face with Argyll's army at Sheriffmuir. The battle that followed was a mess, in the sense that the Jacobite right wing scattered Argyll's left wing while Argyll's right wing repelled the Jacobite left wing. Mar retreated to Perth, and what was left of Argyll's force still blocked the road to the south.

All this was over before James finally turned up in Scotland. In spirit, the Jacobite cause was defeated. And James was not the kind of leader who could rekindle the spirit. The reality of war was not at all the same as dreams of triumph, and he agreed that Perth should be abandoned and that his troops should move north. At Montrose, he quietly disappeared and took a ship back to exile. He had never even addressed his loyal troops, and with his departure, they gave up and went home.

There was another try in 1719, when the Pretender had acquired support from Spain. A small Spanish force was sent to Scotland while a larger fleet prepared to attack England. The larger force was driven back by the weather, while the contingent in Scotland was quite easily rounded up.

Thereafter the Government found a new weapon against rebellion – Field Marshal Wade's roads. The old Highland tracks favoured Highlander guerrilla tactics because they were incapable of taking artillery. With a brand new road network – 250 miles of them in a dozen years, with bridges to link them and a series of forts and barracks to provide bases for garrisons – the Highlands were open to the forces of law and order.

Thirty years after James's abortive visit, his son took the scene. Charles Edward Stuart, Bonnie Prince Charlie, the Young Chevalier, was an altogether more convincing leader of men than his father had been. He is the subject of all those romantic songs and stories, and he was indeed a commanding and romantic figure, who found his way by sea to the Hebrides to lead his own rebellion.

Where the Highland chiefs were cautious and reluctant, he charmed them into joining him. Men flocked to his standard. It has been said that when he arrived in Britain – he was only 25 – he could scarcely speak English. This is improbable. He was a very bright child, and though raised in Italy had become fluent in English and French, as well as Italian. He was tall, handsome and a natural athlete.

It was not easy. When he left the Islands and landed in Moidart, he had only seven sup-

porters. Cameron of Lochiel determined to persuade Charles to give up the idea, but made the mistake of meeting him personally. He was totally won over by the young man's determination, called his clansmen to join the fight, and the rebel army snowballed.

Above: The Earl of Mar, 'Bobbing John', raises the Jacobite standard in 1715.

Below: Mar's opponent in the drawn Battle of Sheriffmuir, John 2nd Duke of Argyll seen here in the painting by William Aikman.

JOHN, DUKE OF
ARGYLL & GREENWICH.

They took over Perth, advanced to Edinburgh, and took it with little difficulty. Government troops under John Cope did their best, but the Jacobites were unbeatable. Faced with cavalry, their response was to strike the horses' noses, a flagrant departure from the polite rules of combat, and send them stampeding backwards. Cope's force was finally routed by a surprise dawn attack on his camp at Prestonpans.

The young prince was the effective master of Scotland. He spent rather a long time in simply enjoying the delights of the Scottish capital and the adulation of its citizens, but he finally moved. He occupied Manchester and was received with wild enthusiasm by the citizens. The same thing happened in Derby.

Charles wanted to move right on to London. The Government there was terrified, King George was thinking of fleeing the country. But Lord George Murray, one of the Prince's generals, advised caution, advised returning to Scotland, advised consolidating. So they returned to Scotland. It is useless to conjecture on what an advance on London might have achieved. The rebellion was over once the decision was made.

The rebels were pursued by government

troops under the Duke of Cumberland, a capable and ruthless commander whose name is remembered by the English in the flower Sweet William, and by the Scots as Butcher Cumberland. The final battle was at Culloden, near Inverness, and it was a slaughter.

Above: Ruthven Barracks, one of the forts built after the '15 to help subdue the Highlands.

Below: The Porteous Riot in Edinburgh in 1736, following trouble with the collection of 'English' taxes.

Cumberland had put out a forged order suggesting that the rebel policy was to take no prisoners and to spare no life. That was his own policy when he triumphed at Culloden. Every available survivor was killed. And after the battle, Cumberland's men combed the Highlands and murdered anybody – man, woman or child – who even looked like an admirer of the Prince.

Charles escaped, to live the life of a hunted beast, sleeping rough, starving, and chilled by the bleak Scottish winter. There was a price of £30,000 on his head. No Highlander ever thought of collecting it.

No matter how we view the Stuarts or their cause, his story was the genuine stuff of drama and romance. He was hardly more than a boy. There is no evidence that he was interested in romantic adventure in the conventional sense, and some amateur psychologists have tried to find something suspicious about that. But people of both sexes were captivated by his

Above: The Battle of Prestonpans, September 1745. The Highland army routed Sir John Cope's force with a surprise dawn attack. The flight of Cope's army is remembered in the song *Hey Jonnie Cope.*

Below: The final defeat of the Jacobites at Culloden, 16 April 1746.

Far left: Disbanded by John Pettie, a disillusioned Highland warrior returns home.

Left: The Jacobite heroine Flora MacDonald painted in 1747 by Richard Wilson.

Below: Prince Charles Edward Stuart, Bonnie Prince Charlie by an unknown artist after Louis Blanchet.

charm and courage, and refusal to complain about his miserable plight. It was undoubtedly the chill climate of his hunted winter in Scotland that turned his taste to whisky and other liquor, a habit he found hard to abandon, later.

During his desperate wanderings, he met on the Isle of Uist Flora MacDonald, who agreed to take him to her family home on the Isle of Skye. For concealment, he wore women's clothes and was known as Betty Burke, servant to Flora. Even on Skye, he was in danger of discovery. He did not make a convincing maidservant. A real servant complained to Flora, 'I have never seen such a tall, impudent jaud in all my life. See what long strides she takes.' He was ill, he was in despair. But Flora watched over him, and got him a ship back to the mainland and to further weeks of wretched hiding until he finally found passage to France, on a frigate, ironically named *l'Heureux* (the Happy One).

Flora's part was purely patriotic. Their farewell was that of two trusting comrades in arms. She was soon arrested and taken to the Tower of London, but freed under an amnesty in 1747, and three years later, she married.

The '45, as the whole episode became known, is positively the end of the Stuart connection with Scotland, one might think. It is not, of course. Charles lived in exile, where he became a nuisance. He drank, he had mistresses, he plotted vaguely and unsuccessfully. He had a daughter by one of the mistresses, Clementina Walkinshaw, who left him, weary of his drunkenness and violence. He married Louise, daughter of the Princess de Stolberg, and sank into a sick, obese old age. He died in 1788, mourned by almost nobody. Now, positively, we might say, the end of ane auld sang.

5 The Enlightenment

I N EDINBURGH in 1696, Thomas Aikenhead, a student, was tried for blasphemy, convicted and executed. He had denied the divinity of Christ.

The astonishing element in this incident is that it happened at a time which can now be seen as the prelude to the sudden flowering of liberal philosophy and scientific and artistic achievement known as the Scottish Enlightenment. The eighteenth century saw clergymen themselves being encouraged to adventure in contemplations philosophical and theological.

It is always dangerous to look back in time and see a golden age, and the Edinburgh of that century had its dark spots of filth and poverty and hunger and drunkenness – the drunkenness even involving children. It was a congested and foul-smelling city with plenty of the ancient sins.

Nevertheless, it was also the setting for the marvellous spectacle of the Enlightenment, which was real. The Kirk, which naturally figures in this as in every other aspect of Scottish history, tended to polarise as the century went on, with the Popular party at one end and the Moderate party at the other.

Two things of significance happened in 1712, after the Union of Parliaments. One was the Act of Toleration, which once more permitted Episcopalians freedom of worship, and the use of the English prayer book. Another was the return of patronage in the appointment of Presbyterian ministers, a system which had been scrapped twenty years before. Pulpits were once more in the gift of the local landowners.

The congregations were often in bitter dispute with the landlords, and in general the reason was that the patrons' choice of minister was more liberal than the worshippers liked. The result, however, was that the more open-minded members of the clergy steadily grew in influence, and there is no doubt that the Church made its own contribution to that exhilarating age. The Popular party was thirled to the old ways, to strict regularity and discipline, but it could do little to stem the tide of progress.

The case of the Reverend Robert Wallace is not entirely typical. His private views smack more of our own century than his. But he was not alone. In a letter to a colleague he advised discretion and silence to anyone whose opinions had changed since his original subscription of faith. And he wrote an essay on morality which he decided should not be published, since its contents were 'so contrary to our present notions and manners.'

The manuscript has survived. It is undated, but the letter referred to above was written in 1730 and the essay shows the same spirit. It is entitled 'Of Venery, or of the Commerce of the two Sexes,' and it is worth quoting at length.

'... but in truth love & lust are very nearly allied, & the most bashful virgin or chastest matron has often more lust or inclination to Venery than the greatest prostitute, who often has an aversion to her trade & only consents & submits to the drudgery of the Act in the view of money.'

The reverend gentleman was very dubious about the idea of platonic love.

'Seldom I believe can a man admire the good qualities of a fine woman's mind and conduct without a secret wish to be familiar with her person. Virtue, honour, prudence, may restrain him from any indecency, but his regard is allwayes mixed with something sensuall.

'If his health & the temperament of his body be vigorous he would gladly rush into her embraces. What women feel I know not but perhaps the most bashfull virgin or chastest matron may not be without the same sort of passionate Desires.

'I imagine where ever there is any secret desire after Venery, this desire is moved by every object which has not something so ugly or Disagreeable as is sufficient to extinguish the Desire altogether.

'I think Fornication should be Disscouraged, but be only gently punished. It ought not to be accounted a very great blot even upon a

Above: The poet Allan Ramsay, 1686-1758, by William Aikman. Ramsay was a leading figure in Edinburgh society of his day.

Previous page: The Old Town of Edinburgh from the west in 1781 by Philip Mercier.

woman's character. It would be much better if fornication gave less scandall & there was less jealousy of wives & mistresses.'

The Enlightenment was not, of course, a sexual revolution. But it was an age when a presumably respectable minister could think such thoughts without anguish of conscience. And Wallace also believed that it should be permissible for women to make proposals as well as men.

If his private opinions were not generally held, there was plenty of liberality, or perhaps looseness is a better word. He served as Moderator of the General Assembly of the church, during whose meetings, it was commonly known, the prostitutes of Rose Street enjoyed a boom trade.

We may leave that interesting side issue to look at the general state of higher education as the century started. The universities were in some disorder after a lengthy period of religious strife, and short of money. But they were on the brink of development and expansion which would bring them international respect.

For one thing, Latin was rapidly abandoned as the language of academic lectures. And regenting was abandoned; the system under which a regent taught one class in several subjects, from books of his own choice, sometimes of his own making, and supervised disputations. This was the age when professors became specialists in a single subject.

The Scottish legal system was untouched by the Union. It differed quite widely from the English, was a blend of Roman and canon law,

and had been clarified and codified in 1681. Young lawyers would go to Utrecht, Gronigen or Leyden to enlarge their studies, and their knowledge of the wider world; and this was significant because lawyers dominated Edinburgh society. The Enlightenment embraced Glasgow and Aberdeen, but the capital city was the heart of it.

It penetrated, all the same, to nearly every activity in Scotland, even to agriculture, in which people like John Cockburn of Ormiston, MP, enclosed his lands, arranged instruction for his tenant farmers in improved techniques, and imposed firm regulations. Lord Kames, in Berwickshire, introduced rotation of crops, and was active in the newly formed Honourable Society of Improvers in the Knowledge of Agriculture, which was founded, in Edinburgh, in 1723. The scope of the Enlightenment is well demonstrated by the fact that the poet Allan Ramsay went so far as to compose an ode to this group.

Continue, best of clubs, long to improve
Your native plains, and gain your nation's love
Rouse every lazy laird of each wide field
Than unmanured not half their product yield.

Scottish ideas were rapidly replacing English ideas. The modern threshing machine was developed north of the border. Scotsman James Clark designed the modern horse shoe, superseding the broad dished pattern used throughout Europe, and wrote a seminal book on the prevention of disease incidental to horses.

James Small invented the first modern

Far right: The title page from a publication of the Improvers. Such publications were influential in spreading knowledge of new scientific methods of farming.

Right: Alexander 'Jupiter' Carlyle, 1722-1805, a leader of the Moderate party in the church, who opposed a return to the more extreme Calvinist teachings regarding forms of worship and the conduct of everyday life.

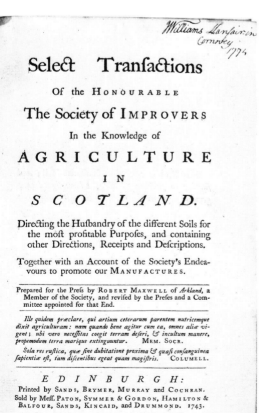

Select Transactions

Of the HONOURABLE

The Society of IMPROVERS

In the Knowledge of

AGRICULTURE

IN

SCOTLAND.

Directing the Husbandry of the different Soils for the most profitable Purposes, and containing other Directions, Receipts and Descriptions.

Together with an Account of the Society's Endeavours to promote our MANUFACTURES.

Prepared for the Press by ROBERT MAXWELL of *Arkland*, a Member of the Society, and revised by the Preses and a Committee appointed for that End.

Ille quidem præclare, qui artium ceterarum parentem nutricemque dixit agriculturam: nam quando bene agitur cum ea, omnes aliæ vigent; ubi vero necessitas coegit terram deseri, & incultum manere, propemodum terra marique extinguuntur. MEM. SOCR.

Sola res rustica, quæ sine dubitatione proxima & quasi consanguinea sapientiæ est, tam discentibus egeat quam magistris. COLUMELL.

EDINBURGH:

Printed by SANDS, BRYMER, MURRAY and COCHRAN. Sold by Mess. PATON, SYMMER & GORDON, HAMILTON & BALFOUR, SANDS, KINCAID, and DRUMMOND. 1743.

plough, which eliminated two oxen from the team. The old runrig system of farming was replaced by enclosed fields. High farming in East Lothian was so successful that it attracted visitors from Europe and America to study it. Dairy farming, the quality of beef, and sheep runs, were all superior to those of England.

There were problems. There were the Levellers, who were incensed by land enclosures and systematically destroyed fences. The Improvements themselves were patchy, and left large areas of the country untouched. There were steady rises in the cost of living, and rural populations were as badly hit as those of the cities.

The general economic growth of the country was prodigious. The population increased by fifty per cent during the century, but the national revenue rose by fifty times. But not everybody shared in the prosperity, and there was a high rate of emigration. By the time of the American War of Independence it was estimated that almost one sixth of the population of the colonies was Scottish or of Scottish descent. Benjamin Franklin reckoned that the proportion in Pennsylvania was fully a third.

In the Scotland they had left behind, we should note that the motive force behind the philosophical explosion was the deep-rooted conviction among intelligent Scots that the most important study a man could undertake was man himself; and specifically, man as a social animal, who could not reach his true potential in isolation but only in membership of the group. This explains why the emphasis of philosophy shifted during the century from psychology to sociology and political economy.

And it was an age of talk, endless, compulsive talk, some of it very good. Clergyman William Robertson was a significant example of the compulsion. Leader of the Moderate party

Left: Dr John Arbuthnot, 1667-1735, friend and collaborator of Swift and Pope, painted here by Kneller.

in the church from the middle of the century, he also became principal of Edinburgh University and served for four years as Moderator of the General Assembly. His term at the university raised it to international status and made it a large contributor to the Enlightenment. He helped to found several of the learned societies of the age, particularly the Select Society and the Royal Society of Edinburgh.

And he talked all the time. He preferred the company of men to that of women. His friends suggested that was because women might out-talk him. His friends sometimes also avoided him because they heard him repeat himself so often.

But his thrust was always to open out the horizons of thought, to make any idea acceptable and discussable. The interesting thing is that the Church, which so recently had been ready and willing to have a young heretic killed, was immersed in the excitements of the new age. One reason was that young men whose families were not rich could aim at the Church as a livelihood.

A man who wanted to write, but could not live by his writing, could make a good living in the church and write at his leisure. The pay was good, compared with that of schoolmasters, though not with that of university professors. No matter. The pulpit could be a halfway house to a university post, and not always in the Divinity faculties. We have mentioned Robert Wallace and his liberal, even shocking views on morality. There was also Alexander Carlyle, nicknamed Jupiter, who passed a lot of his time in the inns of Edinburgh with his friends.

Certainly he was not the average minister. He scandalised his parish elders by attending the theater, a house of the devil, he read Hume, Tobias Smollett and other Scottish writers,

Left: William Hunter, 1718-83, is remembered as a pioneer in obstetrics and gynaecology. He trained initially in Edinburgh but gained his greatest fame (and fortune) in London. The Hunterian Art Gallery at Glasgow University where this painting by Reynolds can be seen, is named for him following a bequest he made to the university.

played cards, was a clubman, and an authority on burgundy.

In short, if we imagine that the Church of Scotland was dour, repressive and conservative, we have to recognise that an important wing was well into the new liberalism. John Home, another clergyman, gave enthusiastic encouragement to James Macpherson in the publication of his translations of Gaelic poems. There is a lot of doubt as to whether they were translations or simply inventions. Macpherson was very coy about showing anybody the originals.

That was not really important. The end product was what mattered, and it put Macpherson triumphantly on the European stage. Enthusiastic readers of his Ossianic pieces included Goethe – himself a giant and not a man to be easily impressed – Schiller, Blake, Coleridge, Scott, Byron, Diderot. The young Napoleon carried an Italian translation of Macpherson's work with him everywhere, and considered him the superior of Homer.

The Reverend John Home himself is a delightful example of the cleric who was not to be confined by outworn intellectual constraints. He didn't merely like the theatre, he wrote for it, the sizeable romance *Douglas*.

When he proposed to have it produced on stage, there was uproar among conservative churchmen, who still regarded the theatre as a gross immorality. Worse, the cast was to include some of the great names of the Enlightenment: David Hume, Jupiter Carlyle, Adam Ferguson, and Home himself. Excommunication was threatened.

The play went on, all the same, and was rapturously received in Edinburgh. Home became known as the Scottish Shakespeare, the success was repeated in London, and the piece

Left: Professor Francis Hutcheson, 1694-1746, a leading liberal thinker, was an important influence on the young Adam Smith at Glasgow University. Hutcheson is seen here in the portrait by Allan Ramsay, 1713-84, son of the poet of the same name, who was the leading Scottish portraitist of his time.

was performed regularly for fifty years in America. Some critics hailed it as the perfect example of the romance genre.

(To the modern mind, it might be less than totally perfect. It concerns the grief of Lady Randolph, who tells her maid at immense length about the disappearance of her infant son twenty years previously; after which a 20-year-old youth remarkably resembling her long-lost lover turns up by chance at the castle, at the same time as a villainous seducer whose motives are obscure. Virtually everybody in the cast meets a violent death. Eighteenth century audiences had strong constitutions.)

Judgement of works of art is, of course, subjective. *Douglas* had social importance in helping to make drama a respectable and acceptable part of life in that buoyant era.

This era also included the famous Robert Burns, who is treated elsewhere in this book. Far from being an illiterate ploughboy, he had a sound education and no feelings of inferiority when he visited Edinburgh in its heyday and met the great and famous of that time. He was part of it all.

As a postscript, we may add that Burns' work was touched by one of the slightly absurd preoccupations of Edinburgh's intellectual community: the contempt for the Scots language. His visit to Edinburgh, and his platonic relationship with one Mrs Mclehose, 'Clarinda', induced him to write some pieces in 'pure' English rather than his own vigorous Scots. A statement by the Select Society of Edinburgh was quite adamant about it.

'Gentlemen educated in Scotland have long been sensible of the disadvantage under which they labour, from their imperfect knowledge of the ENGLISH tongue, and the impropriety with which they speak it.'

Left: Self-portrait by Sir Henry Raeburn, 1756-1823.

The Society had regular lectures on proper English elocution. Modern students of diachronic linguistics, the study of language as a live and constantly evolving organism, may find this bizarre; the heresy that one particular language, or even one particular dialect, is by divine ordinance superior to another. But it was the view of David Hume, and certainly of Adam Smith, who spoke several European languages fluently but was deeply ashamed of his own, and even felt that Doctor Samuel Johnson had not been sufficiently rigorous in excluding low-class words from his dictionary of the English language.

The giants of the Enlightenment period were in one sense turning their backs on their native culture. They dismissed Robert Fergusson, who wrote in Scots, and preferred such poets as Thomas Blacklock and William Wilkie, the farmer poet whose epic poem *Epiconiad* was greatly praised. The work of both men, like that of John Home but not Fergusson, has disappeared leaving little trace.

Walter Scott was a latecomer on the Enlightenment scene, born in 1771, when many of the titans had done their work and passed on. But in a way, his life was a climax to an exciting drama, and with his death in 1832 the golden age was really over. He was created by the Enlightenment. His finest work, in fact, was wrought from Scottish history within the memory of his elders. And his feelings were always ambivalent in his best novels, welcoming a new commercial future for Scotland and shedding a tear for the vanished, crazy glory of the Stuarts. Scott re-invented the lost Scotland of the Stuarts, the clans, the wild

Left: The Reverend John Home, 1722-1808, author of the epic play 'Douglas', now almost forgotten but a dazzling success in its own time. A performance of the play is once said to have inspired the splendid remark 'whaur's yer Wullie Shakespeare noo?' from a member of the audience.

romance. He created the legend of Scotland and imposed it on the literate world. His books would now be classed as blockbusters.

The real glory of the age, of course, was not merely in its writers, or its innovators, but in the feverish spread of ideas among all the active groups, all of them determined to be 'complete men' on the model proclaimed by the thirteenth century genius Roger Bacon. They were concerned not only with their activities, in literature, law, religion or anything else, but with finding a total view of mankind.

Francis Hutcheson, son of a Presbyterian minister in Northern Ireland, and who taught

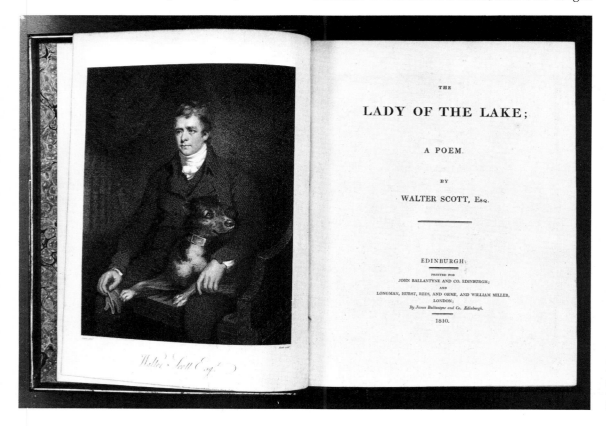

Left: The title page of the first edition of Scott's *Lady of the Lake* with a portrait of the author. Scott's novels did much to popularise the romantic view of Scottish history.

in Dublin before being elected to the chair of moral philosophy at Glasgow University, was a spearhead of the force for liberal thought and got into trouble for it. His passion in life was to understand the nature of morality. Among other things, he dismissed the popular view that people could discover moral laws by the use of reason, and preferred to see men as possessing a moral sense which responded to moral goodness with pleasure.

He studied, not always consistently, the distinction between judging actions according to their motives or according to their results, and sometimes seemed to think their results as more important, using such phrases as 'the general interests of mankind,' and 'the greatest happiness of the greatest number.' This may seem like a mere philosophical quibble, but it mattered to him, and to other contemporaries.

Everything mattered, in fact. One of the implications of his theories was an optimism about the future progress of man as a moral animal, an idea which clashes head-on with the doctrine of original sin, and he was arraigned before the Presbytery of Glasgow for this heresy, for teaching 'the following two false and dangerous doctrines: first, that the standard of moral goodness was the promotion of the happiness of others; and second, that we could have a knowledge of good and evil without and prior to a knowledge of God.'

Unlike that unfortunate student mentioned earlier, he was able to defend himself, the charges were dropped, and he was able to carry on teaching his Glasgow students, who were enthusiastic supporters. This was in 1738, less than half a century after the execution of Thomas Aikenhead.

Hutcheson's philosophy spilled over into a political view of society. He was against authoritarian government, either in society or in the family, championed the rights of married women and proposed to limit the rights of parents over their children. He was for a balanced liberal society in which authority was restricted by law, he favoured the right to political resistance, and in fact believed that people as a whole were too tame and tractable. The essay containing these views was prophetic. It was written twenty years before the American colonists chose the path of political resistance to an over-authoritarian British government.

The enthusiastic hunt for the meaning of things was never an enclosed activity. The speculative work of English figures such as John Locke, Bishop Berkeley and Isaac Newton were eagerly digested and supported or questioned. Berkeley's work was probably more discussed in Scotland than in England, by students as well as the leaders in the field. It was a merry mental battlefield.

Readers need not burden themselves with the inner meaning of the philosophies, unless

they are so inclined. What was important was the fervour with which Scottish thinkers threw themselves into those profound and tenuous contradictions. Members of the Rankenian Club, one of the host of organisations springing up in Edinburgh, corresponded with the good Bishop, who answered regularly in polite terms which ingeniously evaded the consequences of his theories listed by the Rankenians.

The hyperactive minds of the time included, of course, Adam Smith and David Hume, who have been discussed in another chapter. But it is clear that they were not giants among pigmies, rather the finest of a fine breed.

Colin McLaurin, a Rankenian Club member and sharp critic of Berkeley, was primarily, in fact, a mathematician, who produced important and original extensions to the Newtonian calculus and geometry. His work is still taught, and even a brief summary of it is daunting to the layman – a system of generating conics, a method for distinguishing between maxima and minima (in the theory of the multiple points of curves) and a formulation of a concept of level surfaces.

Alongside such people was arising a new generation, and a new enlightenment, in medicine and other sciences. James Douglas raised the practice of anatomy; James Ferguson designed the orrery (a mechanical model of the heavenly bodies); James Short developed parabolic mirrors for telescopes.

Edinburgh University certainly gave the finest medical training in Britain, possibly in the world. Three Alexander Monros, father, son and grandson, were outstanding, holding

Left: Alexander Monro, 'Primus', the first of the remarkable succession of medical professors.

successively the chair of anatomy and surgery. The first defined the relationship of jaundice to the bile tract and made important improvements to surgical instruments and procedures. He found enough spare energy to improve the university physically to make it more attractive to students from North America, and to open its doors to dissenters from the Anglican High Church.

The second Monro wrote three treatises on the brain, the eye and the ear, was the first doctor to use the stomach pump to puncture, surgically, a body cavity in order to drain fluid, and he produced a significant original work on the functions of the nervous system. His course on comparative anatomy was so attractive to students that he had four times as many earning medical degrees as had done a few decades before.

The grandson Alexander was less outstand-

ing in originality, but a superb teacher – his pupils included Sir Humphry Davy and Charles Darwin.

There was also William Cullen, professor of chemistry and later professor of theoretical physics. He did an Augean Stables clean-out of obsolete pharmaceutical formulae, and compiled a Materia Medica Catalogue in 1776 which was a revolutionary advance. His student Joseph Black is regarded as the virtual inventor of modern chemistry. He discovered how carbon dioxide was formed, defined latent heat and specific heat.

And in another typical example of intellectual cross-pollination, Black financed James Watt's work on the steam engine. Watt had heard Black lecture on latent heat, absorbed the knowledge and applied it when he was repairing a specimen of the fairly primitive Newcomen engine, which wasted heat prodigally.

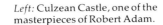

Left: Culzean Castle, one of the masterpieces of Robert Adam.

From his brilliant conception of a separate condenser, he went on, of course, to produce a huge list of other inventions.

The list of scientific and medical pioneers stuns the imagination. John Brown discredited the universal cure-all of blood-letting; James Carmichael Smyth found that nitrous acid gas could inhibit the spread of infection in fever cases. Sir John Pringle transformed military medical practice.

Gynaecology in modern terms was literally invented by William Hunter, whose brother John founded scientific surgery. Thomas Charles Hope identified the new element strontium. His father (and this demonstrates again the wide-ranging versatility of the age) had founded the new Edinburgh Botanic Gardens.

In the middle of all this, the Edinburgh publisher Archibald Constable launched his own contribution to enlightenment: the *Encyclopaedia Britannica*. From a three-volume edition in 1771 it grew to a ten-volume edition in 1778. The Scottish publishing industry became leader in dictionaries and atlases. And its sheer industry was reflected in the acceleration of the country's paper-making industry. Towards the end of the century, mills sprang up in Berwickshire, Midlothian, Dunbartonshire, Perth, Kirkcudbright, five around the village of Lasswade. In Edinburgh there were twelve.

Libraries appeared everywhere, not merely in the cities, and the common man in Scotland was a voracious reader, a participant in the Enlightenment.

And printing went hand in hand with the visual arts. Glasgow printers and booksellers, the Foulis brothers, whose fine printing was unrivalled throughout Britain, produced books of art that were works of art in themselves, and

Below: The fine proportions of the New Town in Edinburgh remain a delight to any visitor to the city.

Robert opened an academy to teach the fine arts. He had his own big collection of old masters, drawings and engravings.

In Edinburgh, the Select Society awarded prizes for drawings of flowers and fruit. In 1760 the Board of Trustees for Improving Fisheries and Manufactures set up in Edinburgh the first school of design in Britain.

Allan Ramsay, poet and bookseller, had a son Allan who in turn dominated Scottish portrait painting, replacing the Jacobean style derived from Van Dyck and absorbing the rococo style of Italy and France. When he moved to London he stood out like an eminence, and George III on his accession appointed him painter-in-ordinary to the king. The portrait of the king and Queen Charlotte was accepted as the official version and widely reproduced.

His portrait of David Hume had no philosophical pretensions about it, but brought the essential quality of the sitter – his unquenchable amiability. Everybody liked Hume, and the Ramsay version helps to explain his popularity as a person.

Henry Raeburn is best known today among the limners of his time, and his Highland chieftain portraits, like The MacNab, Alastair Macdonald of Glengarry and the Marquis of Bute are familiar all over the world, as is his action shot of the Reverend Robert Walker absent-mindedly ice-skating. Raeburn also made his own contribution to the rise of Edinburgh's New Town, by producing exactly the kind of paintings that its citizens would proudly display. There were, of course, architects; and architects of world stature like the Adam brothers. Many of them studied in Rome, including the Adams, and Colen Campbell, the man who imposed the Palladian style

Encyclopædia Britannica;

OR, A

DICTIONARY

OF

ARTS and SCIENCES,

COMPILED UPON A NEW PLAN.

IN WHICH

The different SCIENCES and ARTS are digested into distinct Treatises or Systems;

AND

The various TECHNICAL TERMS, &c. are explained as they occur in the order of the Alphabet.

ILLUSTRATED WITH ONE HUNDRED AND SIXTY COPPERPLATES.

By a SOCIETY of GENTLEMEN in SCOTLAND.

IN THREE VOLUMES.

VOL. I.

EDINBURGH:

Printed for A. BELL and C. MACFARQUHAR;
And sold by COLIN MACFARQUHAR, at his Printing-office, Nicolson-street.

M.DCC.LXXI.

on the country seats of England as well as Scotland, including such fine buildings as Wansted House in Essex, Houghton Hall, Mereworth Castle and Newby.

Since we are still dealing with Scotland, we are not surprised that the Campbell style was not meekly accepted by others. Sir William Chambers and Robert Adam introduced their own revolution of neo-Classicism. Chambers designed the Chinese pagoda for Kew Gardens, and later Somerset House. Adam gave us Culzean Castle, Adelphi Terrace in London, the Duke of Northumberland's Syon House, Register House in Edinburgh, and Edinburgh University, which was unfinished at his death. His Charlotte Square in Edinburgh is one of the quiet delights of that delightful city. Culzean Castle is simply magnificent.

Charlotte Square was part of Edinburgh's New Town. Some say that the New Town was not a part of the Enlightenment, but like the intellectual ferment, it was a parallel and practical striving for perfection. The old city of Edinburgh was bordered on its north side by a

Above: The title page of the first edition of the *Encyclopaedia Britannica.* As the small print at the bottom shows, it was a production of an Edinburgh society.

Left: The great architect Robert Adam.

loch, across which a bridge was built to give access to the land on the north side. Then the loch itself was drained, and in 1767 the New Town began to rise.

James Craig, in overall charge, had the idea that the development should make a political statement of the unity of Scotland and England. City squares were named for the patron saints, Andrew and George, connected with a street named for King George, and flanked by narrower streets called after the national emblems, Thistle Street and Rose Street. Some people at the time dismissed the whole thing as a draughty parallelogram. It was a good ground for the Scottish tradition of disputation.

Sir Henry Cockburn, the judge, wrote later of his dislike of 'long straight lines of street, divided to an inch, and all to the same number of inches, by rectangular intersection, every house being an exact duplicate of its neighbour with a dexterous avoidance, as if from horror, of every ornament or excrescence by which the slightest break might vary the surface. What a site did nature give us for our New Town. Yet what insignificance in its plan. What poverty in all its details.'

He also complained bitterly that Edinburgh had been graced with fine trees, and that the builders were apparently dead against trees which might obscure the view of their new frontages. It should be recorded that trees have re-established themselves here and there.

The development brought an important social change. In old Edinburgh, people of all classes could be found living in the same tenements. It soon became clear that the wealthier, the lawyers in particular, were moving to the New Town and leaving the lower classes in the Old. In 1793, a wheelwright owned a house in the Old Town which a century before had belonged to the Duke of Douglas.

It is still possible, for anyone of imagination, to catch a whiff, in the Old Town and the New Town, of that magic age when Edinburgh was the Athens of the North. And the magic was not only the discoveries and achievements of outstanding individual talents. It was the interminable talk, the argument, the abandonment of barriers between different disciplines. Science, literature, medicine, philosophy, law, art, were all combined in a heady Scotch broth of the mind.

Talking, drinking, dancing, filling the clubs that proliferated to decide finally the secret of the human race; these were the delights of the Enlightenment. The world of the mind has never been the same since.

Below: James Craig's plan for the New Town of Edinburgh.

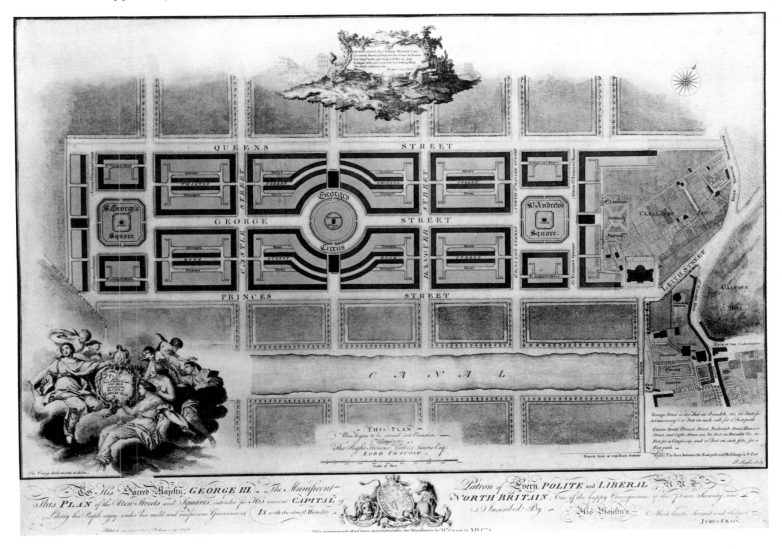

6 The Industrial Revolution

THE MOVE from traditional craft industries to mechanised manufacture which we know as the First Industrial Revolution transformed the face and nature of Scotland. But just as significantly, Scotland was an innovator in that revolution, on a scale away out of proportion to its size and population.

The sheer size of the change can be explained partly by the natural advantages of having raw materials, coal and iron, easily accessible; but there was something more than that, a sudden dramatic flowering of inventive and entrepreneurial genius, something like a sudden mutation in a species that transforms its relationship with the environment. Overnight, it seemed, the country was throwing up men of ability and foresight with the urge to convert old problems into new riches.

A lot of this frenzied activity centred on the River Clyde, which, if we look back now, seems a very improbable site for a great industry. It was shallow and broad, useless for navigation except by little rowing-boats. But Clydesiders dreamed dreams. As long ago as 1566 there was an optimistic scheme to dredge a channel deep enough for bigger craft, but it was a flop. The silt simply slid back into the channel and blocked it.

All that could be done was to establish a seaport well down the river, and Port Glasgow was accordingly established in 1658.

However, the dreamers were not finished. In 1758 John Smeaton made a close survey of the river, and proposed a dam to raise the level of the water. Like the dredging scheme before it, the dam idea petered out. John Golborne came along ten years later with a completely contradictory idea. If jetties were built, sticking out into the stream on both sides, they would slow down the flow near the banks and speed it up in the middle so that it would scour the bed on its way to the sea.

This plan did work. More than two hundred jetties were built. The centre of the stream became navigable. Later the jetties were joined together. It is hard to imagine, looking at the narrow river today, that it has been virtually man-made from a sprawling shallow estuary.

It should be remembered that in the social sense, this was a very primitive country. In the seventeenth century, coal miners – for the coal industry was already well launched – were literally slaves, bound to their masters for life; and slaves of both sexes, at that, and of all ages from tiny children up. Various laws were introduced to ease their lot, but it wasn't until an act of 1799 that they became free people, entitled to leave their jobs like everybody else.

It was only from then that the industry really started to develop its scale. In 1814, the country consumed something over two million tons. Half a century later the production was up to twenty million tons.

The new industries developed sometimes in partnership, sometimes independently. Among the early starters was wool, which got off the ground in the second half of the eighteenth century, and it is interesting to note that it entered a boom in part through the casual intervention of Walter Scott, the great romantic novelist whose popularity was worldwide, and who chose to wear trousers made of wool manufactured in his native Border country. He gave wool glamour and the world hurried to adopt it.

The stuff, incidentally, was called tweel, the Scots version of twill. Somebody in London misread the word as tweed, possibly confusing it with the Border River Tweed, and tweed it is to this day, the truly aristocratic material for sports coats.

The eighteenth century also saw the rise of the linen and tobacco industries. Linen, imported from Ireland and Europe to be processed and exported, rose rapidly to become the country's most important manufactured export, and while it benefited from new industrial techniques, it also produced a modern finance-capitalism structure with the founding of the British Linen Company (later the British Linen Bank) in 1746. By 1771, Glasgow was supreme in Britain as the centre of linen, but a

Above: James Watt, the mechanical genius whose improvements to the existing clumsy steam engines helped spark off the industrial revolution.

Previous page: A deceptively pastoral scene but a clear token of things to come, Knox's painting *First Steamboat on the Clyde*.

few years later it would be replaced by cotton, which apart from sporadic crises like the famine produced by the American Civil War was to prosper into the beginning of the twentieth century.

The rise of the tobacco industry began around 1745, and it was prodigious. It made millionaires, known in Glasgow as the Tobacco Lords, and they thought so much of themselves that when they took a stroll of a morning on the Plainstanes, near Glasgow Cross, they would not tolerate any lesser creature walking on the same paving stones.

In its thirty great years, it came to account for 38 per cent of all Scottish imports, and 56 per cent of all Scottish exports. The thirty-year period ended in 1775, when the city bought 40 million pounds of raw tobacco. The weed was imported, of course, from the colonies as Virginia, and one year later those colonies were to decide on no taxation without representation, and launch the American War of Independence. Even after the war was over, the imports dropped to a few hundred thousand pounds, and the trade never really recovered.

If these tales suggest a constant experience of disaster and gloom, the impression is misleading. Between the troughs, the peaks were exhilarating, and the sheer uncertainty of life had created a spirit of enormous resilience in the city of Glasgow which strangers find striking to this day. Hard times had the interesting effect of creating a sense of unity, of interdependence ('it's the poor that help the poor'), and a tough, fairly black sense of humour which is proof against catastrophe.

The cotton industry was not confined to Glasgow. It began on any scale, in fact, in the improbable location of Rothesay, now a pleasant little holiday town on the Island of Bute, in the Firth of Clyde. It had the first mill of any size in 1779, with a thousand spindles. Inside a few years, the cotton business had proliferated to become Scotland's number one industry; and when we recall the slavery of the coal miners, it is also interesting that among the mill owners who sprang into prominence was David Dale, who is a story in himself.

In an age when we may assume (and often rightly) that the object of the employing classes was to get the maximum labour for the minimum money, Dale was distinctly a misfit. Born in humble circumstances in Ayrshire, he served an apprenticeship as a weaver, spent some time as a buyer of linen yarn, and was later a successful importer of foreign yarns. At a significant time in his life he made the acquaintance or Richard Arkwright, the English inventor whose spinning-frame would transform the cotton industry (and incidentally, caused riots among workers who saw it as a threat to employment).

The two men became partners to set up a cotton spinning mill at New Lanark, on the

Left: The pioneer industrialist and social reformer David Dale, 1739-1806.

upper reaches of the River Clyde. It prospered, and Dale prospered with it, but he and his son-in-law Robert Owen, who took over the mill in 1799, were also preoccupied with social justice and the dignity of labour, and had in mind not merely a factory, but a community, an ideal society in miniature, a village which would provide employment and wages and the other amenities such as education by which the

Left: Robert Owen, 1771-1858, painted here by Mary·Ann Knight, was in fact born in Wales but is best known for his association with New Lanark.

labouring force would rise to their full social stature.

It was not exactly a failure. The English poet Southey, taken on a visit by an enthusiastic friend, was completely put off by the complacent paternalism of the experiment, felt that it involved an underlying superiority complex and even an unacknowledged contempt for the lower orders. But to many social reformers, even down to this day, it is regarded as a vision of the good society, and it has been affectionately preserved as a monument to idealism.

Perhaps it was Owen's lofty determination to teach his workpeople the virtues of thrift, cleanliness and good order that put Southey off. But Owen's visionary quality was never to leave him. As well as the New Lanark project, he set up an ideal socialist community in New Harmony, in Indiana, and others elsewhere. They failed, largely because he had overlooked

the incurable complexities of human nature. The American experiment fell to pieces because its doctrine of brotherly and sisterly love and universal care attracted loafers and bums who liked the idea of being taken care of.

The family did make some contribution to America, all the same. Robert's son, also Robert, settled in the country when New Harmony collapsed, became a member of the Indiana legislature and later of Congress, and was chargé d'affaires and later U.S. Minister at Naples. He was an ardent abolitionist, as could be expected. He was also an enthusiastic spiritualist. The Owens had a compulsion to believe in things.

An important element of the times is that the mill at New Lanark employed its own engineers, over eighty of them, to manufacture its machinery on the spot, and this was common before machine-making became the work of

Above: John Glassford and his family, painted by Archibald McLauchlin around 1767. Glassford was one of Glasgow's 'Tobacco Lords' and the city's Glassford Street is named after the family.

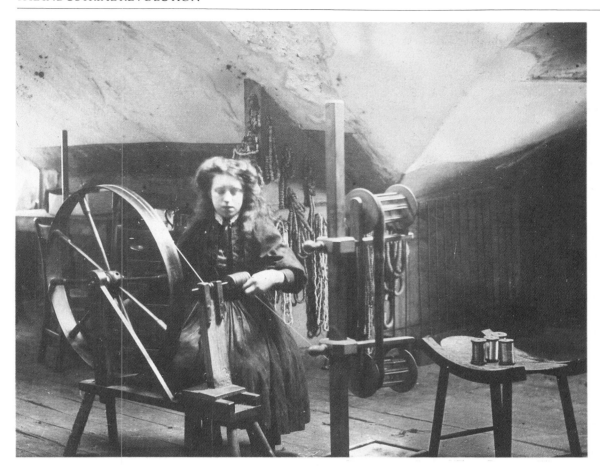

Left: The reality of industrial life was often less comfortable than family portraits suggest: a scene in a Glasgow workshop at the turn of the present century.

Below: The Trongate of Glasgow, painted in 1826 by John Knox. By this time Glasgow had already overtaken Edinburgh as the largest and most productive town in the country.

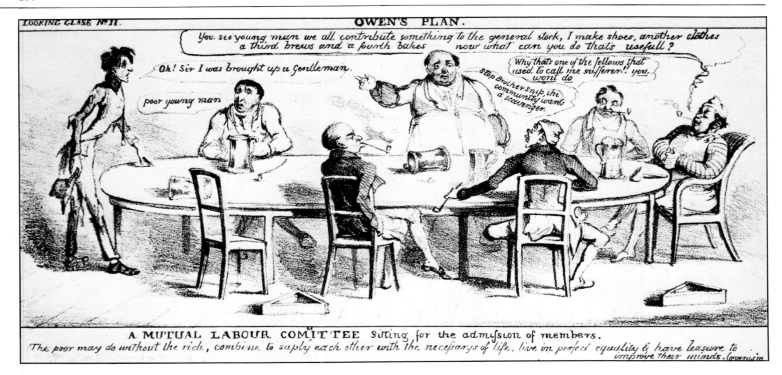

Above: A satirical contemporary view of the prospects for Owen's socialist plans.

specialist companies. The celebrated Templeton carpet factory in Glasgow was making its own looms right into the 1960s.

With the spread of new machinery came social upheaval. The handloom weavers for a long time were an elite, commanding high wages, but as the machines spread they were pushed to the edge of the industry and their average wage fell to a quarter. At their peak they could earn forty shillings a week, which is a meaningless statement in modern monetary terms, but was princely in its context. And as we have seen, the American Civil War in 1861 was the end of the industry's great days.

Dundee, on the East Coast, was second only to Glasgow in its industrial energy, and principally in jute, which also produced its inventive genius in the person of Peter Carmichael, a local who had studied the manufacture of textile machinery and became general manager of the city's biggest jute company, Baxter's, at the age of twenty-four, to preside over a buoyant expansion. By 1850 the industry was in such boom times that it was said anybody who could buy or rent a tumbledown mill could make a fortune.

The boom, naturally, collapsed, but, as elsewhere in the world, wars were good for business, and the city had rich times during the Crimean War, supplying material for tents, sails and gun covers. It had another fillip supplying stuff to the North during the American Civil War.

Dundee was built, it was said, on jute, jam and journalism. The jute is gone. The jam still flourishes with Keiller's high-quality preserves. The journalism is a truly remarkable story of Scottish dedication. While other press barons in Britain have looked for their fortunes in London's Fleet Street, the D. C. Thomson

company has throughout its generations stayed rooted to its native Dundee and become rich and successful beyond belief.

It publishes the city's daily paper, the *Courier*, a splendidly old-fashioned and conservative organ which rightly considers Dundee the centre of the world. The story is untrue, but almost credible, that its report of the Titanic disaster was headlined 'City Man Lost at Sea.' D. C. Thomson also publishes *The Sunday Post*, a folksy journal eagerly read by exiled Scots all over the world to give them a unique flavour of the land they have left behind them. For much of its life *The Sunday Post* was so folksy that it was almost possible to read a back number without realising it was out of date. But it is in fact an immensely shrewd operation, changing unnoticeably to meet changing times. It has a circulation of a million and a half, a staggering figure in a nation with a population of under five million.

The family – and it is a family, a dynasty – also puts out a sheaf of children's comic papers which have filled and even shaped the minds of youngsters all over Britain for generations. They are easy to read, wholesome even if some of their cartoon characters are dreadful brats, and ineffably successful. The family, which totally shuns personal publicity and lives quiet and unostentatious lives, has never failed in any new venture. Their offices have been the training ground for many people destined to become great names in national and international journalism, and they go on thriving and providing millions of people with good clean fun.

It is difficult to separate the developments in coal, steam, iron and the railways. They were activities that fed one another and fed on one another. And they grew fast on feeding. The first Carron ironworks was established at the head of the River Forth in 1759. By 1825 there were over 70 foundries in Scotland. They were concentrated mostly in Lanarkshire and Ayrshire, changing the face of the land.

And James Watt, the innovative genius from Greenock, had long since turned steam into a prime mover of prodigious potential. His first engine, in fact, was installed at Carron, in an oddly antiquated context. The Carron works took its power from a water wheel, and the Watt engine was used to pump the water back up into the reservoir.

The engine that powered the early steamship *Comet* had been designed for a similarly mundane job in a factory. Let us get rid of the widespread assumption that Henry Bell invented the steamship with his *Comet*. There was a much earlier little steamboat, the *Charlotte Dundas*, which plied on the Forth and Clyde Canal. It was seen there in 1801, eleven years before the *Comet*, by Robert Fulton, who promptly returned to America to emulate it with his *Clermont*, which plied on the Hudson River, still comfortably in advance of the *Comet*; which incidentally was not invented by Bell, who was merely a progressive businessman. The hull was by Woods of Port Glasgow,

the engine was by John Robertson of Glasgow, and the boiler by David Napier.

Probably the first ever steamboat in the world was an American craft called simply *The Steamboat* as she was the only one in the world. She was made by one John Fitch, and launched into the Delaware in 1790. Fitch either disliked paddle wheels, or had not thought of them, and his craft was propelled by a series of oars at the stern, manipulated by steam power. Her first sailing was announced for 27 July from Philadelphia to Trenton, returning on the following day. It worked, but not very well and very unreliably, and the plan was abandoned.

Bell could at any rate claim to have organised the first steamboat to travel by sea. We may leap ahead to look at the revolution this tiny (40 feet by 10 feet) craft inaugurated, a significant piece of Scotland's social history.

Only a few months after *Comet*'s maiden voyage, the Clyde saw a bigger and stronger paddler, the *Elizabeth*; quickly followed by the *Clyde* and the *Glasgow*. By 1820 there were over a score of passenger and cargo boats, one of the passenger craft plying regularly from Scotland to Londonderry in Northern Ireland.

A fine madness overtook the people of Clydeside. They fell in love with steam, and the

Below: A Glasgow and Clydeside tradition from the earliest days of steam shipping until very recent times, steamers set off taking passengers and holidaymakers for trips 'doon the watter.' This photograph dates from around 1900.

Right: The proud crest on the buildings of the Carron Ironworks, one of the earliest of the developments of the industrial revolution and a recent victim of present industrial problems.

sea, and with speed. Dozens of businessmen invested in paddlers to compete for the passenger trade, and those who chose luxury and comfort for their boats could not take trade from those who had fast boats.

The principal hazard in the early days was bursting boilers. In 1842 the *Telegraph* exploded at Helensburgh, killing more than twenty people. There were many other minor disasters. None of them affected the passion of Glaswegians for a trip 'doon the watter.'

It has even been suggested that the expansion of the Clyde steamer service virtually inaugurated the idea of leaving home for a holiday, certainly among working-class people. The situation is of course ideal, for the Clyde runs into an estuary flanked with majestic hills, etched with sea lochs and scattered with beautiful islands. It still provides the finest yachting water in the world.

The craze certainly brought a shock to the moral and religious principles of old Scotland, because some of the shipowners started to

Below: The engine from the pioneering steamship, the *Comet,* with the engineer, John Robertson, who built the engine to Henry Bell's design.

organise day trips on the Sabbath, an appalling prospect to the virtuous people of Rothesay, where even the pump-wells were padlocked on Saturday nights and left like that till Monday morning, in case some citizen should stain his soul by taking a drink of water from them on a Sunday.

There was at least one pitched battle when the steamer *Emperor* tried to tie up at Luss pier. The laird, Sir James Colquhoun, had ordered that no landing should be permitted, and a little army was posted on the pier to repel visitors. Mooring lines were thrown back on board. The passengers set up a hail of missiles to beat back the defenders, leapt ashore and engaged in hand-to-hand warfare. All the time most of the good people of Luss were at church, hearing the din but missing the entertainment.

Sunday cruises did establish themselves, without further violence. But on any day of the week, speed was still king, and this persisted into the middle of the twentieth century, when there were still two rival companies plying the Firth of Clyde, and staid middle-aged passengers would line the rails and scream to their captain to beat a rival paddler to the pier. And right up to that time there were dozens of paddle steamers carrying packed crowds of holidaymakers to the little holiday towns and villages. The tradition was deeply entrenched.

It was another mechanical device that brought the golden age to an end: the motor car. Now there are only a few workaday passenger and car ferries sailing on the Firth. The motor car, and cheap package holidays to the Continent, rang down the curtain on a great era.

To return to the great 'heavy' developments of iron and steel, we find again the passionate Scottish urge for discovery, for fighting through technical problems, in the story of the Scot James Beaumont Neilson. The human mind is the most baffling of all historical facts to comprehend, and in this man's mind came the revelation of what the engineers called the hot blast. This was concerned with the processing of iron, and it enabled raw coal from the earth to replace the coke that had been needed to do the job. It also reduced the amount of coal needed by two thirds. Neilson had his eureka revelation in 1828, and within ten years, Scotland's production of iron had gone up sixfold.

A few years later, the Reoch brothers had put up the Parkhead forge, in the East End of Glasgow. It was gigantic. For decades it almost made Glasgow's East End a company town, in which people either worked at the forge, or provided housing for people who worked at the forge, or sold them groceries. This was initiated in 1837, and it made the East End of the city. The company had three ten-ton open-hearth furnaces for ship plates and armour plate. It later branched out into shipbuilding at Dalmuir, on the Clyde, after the turn of the century.

It was too big. This is not an exclusively Scottish story, it can be duplicated all over the industrial western world. In boom times, it swelled. When hard times came, it was in deadly trouble. Beardmore's Parkhead Forge, as it had become, was saved by World War I, the Great War, when it was able to get orders for shells, warships, guns, even aero engines. Its later history was to be a frenzied attempt to diversify. After that war it turned to making cars and taxis, worked on diesel engines and other things, and managed to hold on until World War II, when it was needed to make big armaments and small arms.

After that war, the company diversified even more frantically, into surprising things like typewriters, side by side with enormous forgings. In the end, it was too heavy. Hardly a trace remains of that enormous, secretive, enclosed building that dominated the landscape of Glasgow's East End.

The Glasgow area was best known, of course, as the home of great shipbuilding, all the time from the *Comet*, and that industry was legendary. Scottish schoolchildren were brought up on the aphorism that the Clyde made Glasgow, and Glasgow made the Clyde. Glasgow had certainly made the Clyde, had made it navigable, and the skill and the energy were there to make it the cradle of great shipbuilding.

Robert Napier opened a shipyard in Govan in 1841 to make iron ships, an innovation in itself, and he helped to finance Samuel Cunard's North American Royal Mail Steamship Navigation Company. It was the beginning of a fury of shipbuilding and shipowning. In 1887 Sir William Pearce, who had the Fairfields shipbuilding yard in Govan,

Left: James Beaumont Neilson whose invention of the blast furnace in 1828 transformed the iron industry.

founded the Canadian Pacific Steamship line, to be later amalgamated with the Canadian Pacific line. This was a routine story on the Clyde, which provided the ships that took gold-crazed prospectors from the west coast of North America to the Yukon during the gold rush of 1896.

There was a brief step-aside from iron and steam in 1869, when the Dumbarton shipyard Scott and Linton got an order to build the *Cutty Sark*, a sailing clipper designed to work the

Below: The former Templeton's carpet factory in Glasgow, an exuberant statement, built in a supposed Venetian style, of former pride and confidence. The building now houses a number of workshops and small businesses.

China tea trade and compete against the Aberdeen clipper *Thermopylae*, the fastest on the China run. The curious thing is that everybody in Scotland now remembers the *Cutty Sark*, and nobody remembers the *Thermopylae*, but the *Cutty Sark* lost nearly every race. The sentiment surrounding it is a tribute to Glasgow sentimentality against hard facts.

We come into the twentieth century, and the story is quite complicated. The reputation of Clyde shipbuilding stayed stubbornly on. The reality was less marvellous. Ever since the 1890s, the industry had been sliding from its predominance. It had been a great innovative force in shipping, and there is no doubt that the development of a triple-expansion steam engine for ships by Denny of Dumbarton in the 1860s spelt the real death of long-distance sailing ships. But foreign competition was feeling its muscles, and the foreigners had innovations too.

From this point in history, it seems indeed bizarre that the River Clyde should have set itself up as a great world centre of shipbuilding. It really is very narrow, and when enormous ships were built on the Clyde, to be launched into this small river, they had to have thousands of tons of drag chains behind them

to slow down their descent down the slip, otherwise they would have shot across the river and up on to the far bank.

But this system did work quite well. Into the twentieth century, to name but a few specimens, John Brown's of Clydebank produced the three most prestigious ocean queens, the *Queen Mary*, the *Queen Elizabeth*, and the *Queen Elizabeth II*. They were marvellous, and it is possible that their like will not be seen again. But they were a proud goodbye to the greatness of the Clyde as a shipbuilding river. Other nations, with places more conveniently designed than the Clyde for building great ships, were emerging.

Scotland still has shipyards on the Clyde, and elsewhere. They are all in trouble. Shipbuilding in every country in the world has troubles, but the Clyde has serious troubles.

There was a sudden, unexpected, hopeful incident in 1965, an echo of those Owens who wanted to make the workers proud. Robert Owen was a passionate socialist. Iain Stewart, head of a prosperous industrial company in Glasgow, was an incurable conservative, but he too had a vision, about the future of Clyde shipbuilding, and his vision of a new relationship between workers and management encouraged the London government to let him work out an experiment in the threatened Fairfield shipyard in Govan; a scheme to take a new look at how men and management and ships might become compatible.

Stewart, whatever his politics, had seen something that few other people, in manage-

Above: Riveters at work on the liner *Lusitania* in 1905.

Right: Men at work on the frames and keel plates of the *City of Paris* in 1887.

Right: The modern face of Scottish industry, the processing plant for North Sea Gas at Mossmorran in Fife.

Below: The Ravenscraig steel works. When the strip mill at Ravenscraig was opened in 1963 it was among the most modern in Europe but the plant has since suffered, along with the rest of the British steel industry, and the recent closure of the Gartcosh rolling mill has cast a further shadow over Ravenscraig.

ment or trade unions, had faced before: the desperate Scottish passion for confrontation. Given a free hand, but very little money, he attempted to create an Owenish community at Fairfield, but with a hard mind for the balance sheets and industrial survival.

Stewart's idealism, and his personality, had an astonishing response among the workforce at Fairfields. But before the experiment, in consultation, in retraining, in flexibility, could really get started, a socialist government found it more urgent to amalgamate all the shipyards in the upper Clyde. Somehow the experiment was lost. The amalgamated yards were liquidated in 1972, and the great John Brown's yard, home of the ocean queens, was sold to the Texas company Marathon, at a giveaway price, to become a factory for oil rigs.

The decline of shipbuilding is a melancholy memory, especially when we realise that between 1870 and 1913, the Clyde yards produced nearly a fifth of the world's ships. The construction of locomotives for railways was equally a hectic success story. The great locomotive works established at Springburn in Glasgow in 1860 rose to a dominant place on the world scene, and the district of Springburn grew around them into virtually a company town. At the beginning of this century, India had over seven thousand locos and more than half were made in Glasgow.

The decline came soon after the Great War, when there was a sudden industrial boom that lasted hardly a year. The Springburn factory just managed to hold on, and the spectacle of a gigantic locomotive, of a size that dwarfed British engines, was a regular excitement in the 1920s and 1930s as it was hauled through the city streets on its way to the docks to India. In its time, Springburn also exported to Italy, Spain, Sweden and South America.

And there was a more durable boom that started with the second world war and lasted into the fifties. The company was making solid efforts to get up to date by moving from steam to diesel-hydraulic and then diesel-electric. But after that majestic history, it could not come up with a competitive design, and went into bankruptcy.

The cottage industry that grew into a giant and has never lost its strength in Scotland was something more homely and private; Scotch whisky. As long ago as the fifteenth century, the Scots were making 'aqua vitae', the water of life, as an agreeable hobby. As the centuries went on, and the sizeable distilleries appeared, the powerful potion enriched its creators and enriched the country's lore and literature. This was the stuff that was hailed so pungently in Burns' *Tam o' Shanter*.

> Inspiring, bold John Barleycorn!
> What dangers thou canst make us scorn!
> Wi' tippeny (ale), we fear nae evil;
> Wi' usquabae, we'll face the Devil!

As well as making money for the makers, it put great amounts of money into the Government Treasury. Alcohol has always had a

Above: Probably the last great liner to be built on the Clyde, the *Queen Elizabeth II*, seen shortly before her launch.

Above: A Britoil production platform nearing completion at the construction yard at Ardersier near Inverness.

powerful attraction for the tax man. Indeed, there were riots in Glasgow over an increased malt tax in 1725. A local Member of Parliament, Daniel Campbell of Shawfield, had voted in favour of the tax. A mob looted his house and a dozen people were killed in the affray.

A significant consequence is that when the city paid him £9,000 in compensation, he used it to buy the island of Islay, which today produces several of the most prestigious single malt whiskies of Scotland.

Scotch whisky is surrounded by a powerful mystique, and while this may have elements of fantasy, it is still true that it is quite unlike any spirituous drink made anywhere else in the world. And although like other industries it occasionally suffered setbacks in depressed times, it has proved buoyant and triumphant, has been the greatest single British export in terms of money and shows no signs of fading.

The second industrial revolution is still a-borning. The electronics industry is not likely to employ the masses of workers who were needed for the old 'heavies' in Scotland or anywhere else. But in smaller tidy factories from Dundee to the Spango Valley outside Greenock, there are signs of energy and enterprise. Future history will judge their achievements.

In the sixties, the discovery of oil in the North Sea, north-east of the Scottish mainland, produced a dramatic chapter in the land's industrial history. The economy of the Shetland Islands, which took a very independent line in order to channel the profits into its own economy, was transformed. The port of Aberdeen suddenly acquired a new status as the centre of the booming business and other towns on the East Coast had a share of the great construction programmes for oil platforms.

Nationalistic Scots have been disturbed that the huge revenues were simply absorbed into the operations of the Exchequer in London, and that another slump will follow when the oil runs dry. But there are continuing discoveries of deposits in these stormy waters. They provide, at least, a breathing space for a country with a roller-coaster industrial history. What comes next is another matter. This book is concerned with history and not prediction.

ALL THE WAY from Calgacus, the first recorded Scot, away back in Roman times, Scotland has kept throwing up individuals to make marks on the world, for good or ill, and it is not too much to claim that it threw up more than its tiny population could have been expected to. From a few hundred thousand souls to five million, it seemed to incite innovation. Random calculation would never have expected this tiny nation to produce the people who pioneered mathematics, steam power, the bicycle of all things, the detective agency and the detective novel, roads, bridges, anaesthesia, television, economics, the telephone, radar, penicillin and, of course, rebellion.

It is impossible, in a brief history, to list all the geniuses and madmen or women who helped to change the world from the insecure base of Scotland.

John Napier, the Laird of Merchiston, was a bigoted anti-Catholic and wrote Biblical exegeses on St John, but in his sixteenth century time he moonlighted as a mathematical genius and created logarithms. The logarithm is a process for working out stupefying mathematical problems by means of a book of tables, and has gone out of fashion since the introduction of electronic calculators; but it has made life easier for struggling mathematicians for several centuries, and if the world ever runs out of batteries the logarithm will still be to hand.

Adam Smith is an authentic giant. He has been accused of inventing capitalism, unfairly. He simply analysed capitalism, and invented the science (if science it is) of economics. Karl Marx was one of his detractors, but Karl Marx could never have written his own analysis of society without the pioneering work of Smith. Smith's mind was constantly on the boil with

the nature of society, he did original work on *The Theory of Moral Sentiments*, lectured on behaviour in society, jurisprudence and everything else that swam before his inquisitive consciousness. The world's idea of itself has never been the same since. Smith also had the strong moral sense of Scots in his eighteenth century society. It is the duty of a poet, he said once, to write like a gentleman.

Modern readers might find this baffling, but all people are creatures, and prisoners, of their own age, and it no doubt made sense then.

Smith's *Wealth of Nations* is the seminal work from which every book on economics has sprung ever since, so this Scottish genius has much to answer for.

His contemporary and friend, David Hume, was also an intellectual titan, and a man much loved (something not true of every Scottish genius). Born in Edinburgh in 1711, he had a nervous breakdown at the age of eighteen, worked as a clerk, fled to France, and published

Above: The title page of the first edition of Napier's work on logarithms.

Left: John Napier, 1550-1617. As well as inventing logarithms he also sketched ideas for what we would now recognise as the submarine and the tank.

Previous page: The famous meeting in 1871 of David Livingstone (right) and the writer and explorer Henry Stanley.

his master-work, the *Treatise on Human Nature*, when he was twenty-five.

Hume was the original Missourian Scot. 'Show me!' He believed nothing that could not be demonstrated. He threw out the idea of causality, the idea that if we do something, something else will result. For instance, if we throw a stone in the air, it will come down again. The fact that that has happened a billion times, he pointed out, does not mean that it will happen next time. The billion times could be mere coincidence. What could people do with a man like that? They could listen to him. They did not at first, but he had such charm that he wheedled himself into the consciousness of European intellectual life.

Hume worked at the British Embassy in Paris, he knew Jean-Jacques Rousseau, he predicted the American Revolution, and his political essays gave heart to the Founding Fathers. He wrote an English history, and the *Natural History of Religion*, and acres of tightly argued essays on any subject that caught his eye. He made us think.

The restless spirit that has seized so many Scots, perhaps the feeling that the country was too small for them, drove Mungo Park to his desperate adventures in the opening up of Africa, starting in 1795 when he was only in his twenties and already a qualified surgeon. The exploration was picked up half a century later by David Livingstone, and in today's climate it is possible to have reservations about the real value of their travels. Livingstone is conventionally accepted as the great Christianiser of the dark continent, but he was as absorbed in the possibilities of commerce as in religion, and also dedicated, it must be said, to his own fame and glory. We are dubious today about the long-term effects of the European conquest of Africa, and it is interesting, if fruitless, to wonder how the continent would look today if Europe had simply left it alone. But the Scots, once the English had learned to leave them alone, could not help trying to reshape the world.

It is certainly impossible to exaggerate the power that James Watt, the boy from Greenock, exercised over his world. The legend is that he was fascinated by the way the steam from his mother's boiling kettle could actually move a spoon held in his hand. The truth is that in his late twenties he was working as an instrument maker in Glasgow University, when in 1764 he was asked to repair a Newcomen steam engine. He not only repaired it, but saw the possibilities of a much more efficient machine. He devised refinements like a separate condenser, an air pump and other devices, and later moved to England and into partnership with a Midlands engineer to produce the new, the all-powerful steam engine that was going to launch the earth into a new, all-powerful industrial age. He took out a patent for a steam

locomotive in 1784, thirty years before the English pioneer Stephenson actually built his first. Even in retirement, his home was a workshop where he cheerfully played at inventing all kinds of practical wonders. But if he had never produced anything other than the Watt steam engine, his place as a world-shaker would still be solid.

John Loudon McAdam got the world moving in other ways. Born at Ayr in 1756, he emigrated to New York in his twenties, went into business and made his pile, well enough to come back to Ayrshire and buy a big country estate. He might well have lived out the rest of his life enjoying the life of a country gentleman, but he had the old restlessness, and when he moved south, he became surveyor to the Bristol Turnpike Trust at the surprising age of sixty and organised the reconstruction of its roads with splendid efficiency and economy. He was so good that he became a man in demand all over the country.

McAdam's marvellously simple breakthrough – simple after he had demonstrated it – came from his observations of how stones of different sizes on a roadway moved under

Above: John Loudon McAdam, 1756-1836. Roads built according to his ideas transformed communications in country areas of Scotland and elsewhere, to the great benefit of agricultural development.

Left: Thomas Telford, by George Patten. Telford was born a shepherd's son near Langholm and finished his remarkable career as the first president of the Institution of Civil Engineers.

Far left: Adam Smith, 1723-90.

pressure of traffic. His experiments showed that if stones of different sizes were laid in a graduated pattern, the weight of traffic pressed them together more tightly instead of scattering them. McAdam roads were made to last, and the later addition of tar as a binding agent was merely a refinement.

McAdam's contemporary Thomas Telford got Britain moving too. His work in designing bridges for the River Severn were triumphs that led to his plan for the Ellesmere Canal. The government then employed him to report on the state of his native Scotland's communications, and he built the Caledonian Canal, a waterway linking natural lochs right across the land from south-west to north-east. During his career he created an astonishing thousand miles of roadway, and even more astonishing, well over a thousand bridges, including the revolutionary suspension bridge over the Menai Strait; and docks and harbours and houses almost as afterthoughts. He well deserved the poetic title The Colossus of Roads.

Beside such Scots of solid achievement, James Boswell may seem trivial and even contemptible, and that is probably how he saw himself. He is mostly remembered as the toadying friend of Doctor Samuel Johnson, the great dictionary maker, philisopher and writer of prodigious poetry which now reads very prosily. Boswell, son of a puritanical Scottish judge, had to escape to London to indulge his ravenous appetite for loose women and his pathetic hunger for approval by his intellectual superiors.

He underrated himself. His *Life* of Johnson was certainly a sycophantic exercise, consisting of an endless outpouring into his diary of every trifling remark that fell from the great man's lips. He confessed to his patron that he

included all kinds of trivialities in his journal, and Johnson weightily replied that since man is a little creature by nature, nothing is too little for him.

The journal was anything but little. It is perhaps the most penetrating pen portrait of a live man ever written. Johnson was a big figure in his time, but his great dictionary is now no more than a footnote to the history of lexicography, his other writings are disregarded today, and he would be scarcely remembered

Below: A flight of locks on Telford's Caledonian canal.

Right: One of the Victorian era's heroes, David Livingstone, explorer and missionary.

THE LIFE & EXPLORATIONS OF Dr. LIVINGSTONE

BORN AT BLANTYRE, MARCH 19, 1813

DIED IN CENTRAL AFRICA, MAY 4, 1873

AFRICA

14, IVY LANE, LONDON: & NEWCASTLE ON TYNE,

ADAM & Co.

but for the *Life*, in which he comes out fairly
blazing with reality, a three-dimensional,
heavy-breathing, self-indulgent giant. Generations of weary schoolchildren, overlooking the
intellectual power, have accepted him as a
cantankerous old bully; but they have accepted
him as absolutely real and recognisable. James
Boswell's achievement was to give his hero
everlasting life.

Strangely enough, Boswell's other writings,
including the scabrous *London Journal*, and also
including a great pile of material discovered
only in this century (it had been believed that
most of his stuff had been destroyed by his
family to avoid scandal) survives splendidly, is
wonderfully readable and entertaining and
perceptive; so that in a sense he is bigger than
his master. But the *Life of Samuel Johnson* liter-

ally created a new art form, which other writers can only struggle feebly to follow.

The Scot who wrote and lived out his own life is Robert Burns, whose poetry and personality bestride the world. Few admirers of Beethoven could give off-hand the birthday of the great man (16 December 1770). But millions of Burns enthusiasts today have 25 January 1759 engraved on their hearts. It is curious that there is no tradition of Shakespeare birthday dinners, though even some Scots may concede that he was an incomparably greater poet. There are no ritual annual celebrations of Goethe or Dante Alighieri or Pushkin. But in countries all over the globe people gather around 25 January to dine on haggis, mashed potatoes and turnips, declaim the poetry of Burns and drink to his immortal memory.

There are reasons for the distinction. One is that, almost uniquely, Burns wrote straight to the heart, that he wrote about the absolutely ordinary experiences of men and women, but with a power that ennobled those ordinary experiences; the mundane joys and sorrows and triumphs and regrets. Another is that, like Boswell, he conceals nothing of his own failings, but in his verses even the failings become homeric, real life but bigger than life.

Burns was born into the family of a struggling farmer in Ayrshire and spent his early years struggling with the family to drag a living from the land. He married Jean Armour, and died in Dumfries at the age of 37, from the rheumatic fever that had attacked him in youth without being diagnosed. The years between were continuous theatre, tragedy and comedy. From his mid twenties, he poured his heart, and his magical understanding of the human condition, into a cataract of poetry. Before his marriage, he had a long on-and-off affair with Jean, interrupted by his irrepressible passion for other women. He was irresistible to women and hilarious in the company of men. He drank too much, he glorified drink and warned of its perils. He loved too much. He admired moderation and was incapable of moderation.

But nothing, good or bad, that he did was ever done on the sly. His adventures were an open book, he wrote his poetry and he lived it. The adulation offered to him is for the magic of his poetry, but also for being the man many men would like to be but dare not, for being the man many women would like to have known. He was dying when he wrote, in a single day, his masterpiece *Tam o' Shanter*. On the day of his funeral, Jean was giving birth to twins, penniless.

Death has always had a fascination for the Scots, as indeed it has for other people, and as we have seen, its story is plentifully supplied with abrupt terminations of life.

Not always by intent. The Industrial Revolution in itself, and in its time, took a hideous toll of life. The great enterprises designed to make

Above: Robert Burns, Scotland's greatest poet.

the nation rich exacted a terrible price by sucking huge populations, from the countryside, from the Highlands, from Ireland, into the mushrooming cities. While the barons might build great mansions, the immigrants were often crammed into dank, dark and dismal tenements.

During the explosive expansion of the ironworks, the railways, the shipyards, there were some people in the cities living fifteen or twenty to a single room. In Glasgow of the 1830s the death rate was 2½ per cent; not per thousand, but per hundred. Fully half of the city's children died before the age of five. This is hideous without being fascinating. Fascination is reserved for outlandish death by human agency, and the Scottish story is rich in examples quite as bizarre as in any land.

One of the weirdest is the strange case of Sawney Beane. Mr Beane was born outside Edinburgh in the sixteenth century, of poor but honest parents. Not satisfied with poverty or honesty, he ran away in his adolescence to seek his fortune. He soon fell into the company of an evil woman, and together they roamed the country making a bare living from petty theft.

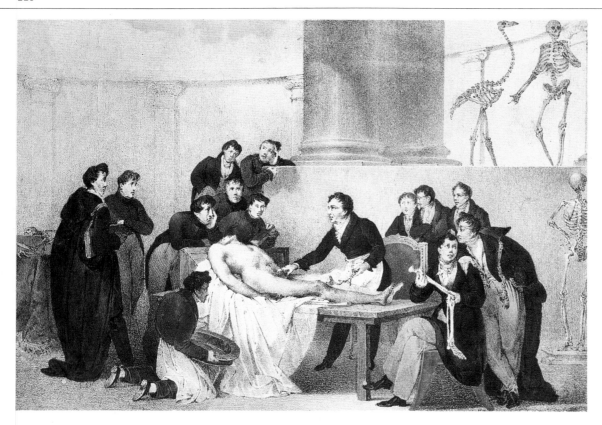

Left: An anatomy lesson in the 1820s. The need for bodies for public dissection in medical schools provided the basis of Burke's and Hare's crimes.

In time they came upon a roomy cave near Bennane Head in Ayrshire, where they established a sort of business and founded a community so self-sufficient that for a quarter of a century they never had to go near a town or village. They simply vanished from society.

Although nobody reported a sighting of them, the district began to acquire an evil reputation as a place where innocent travellers were likely to vanish without trace. There was talk of murder, and according to one report, 'an abundance of innocent travellers and inn-keepers were executed, on suspicion of being the murderers, yet all was in vain.'

It was a dangerous time, when the process of law was often abrupt and arbitrary, and Ayrshire people faced the twin perils of disappearing or being hanged on the basis of rumour. Inn-keepers, being particularly under suspicion began to leave the trade and the district, and with fewer inns available, travellers were forced to make longer journeys between stops, thus falling into graver danger. The magistrates, seeing that the hangings were having no effect, washed their hands of the mystery and left its solution to Providence.

They were rewarded when a man and wife, sharing one horse, were ambushed on the road near Bennane Head by a group of ragged, violent strangers. The wife fell off the horse in fright. Several of the attackers leapt on her at once, stabbed her to death, cut her throat, and before the husband's horrified eyes, began to drink her blood. The very horror gave him strength to draw his sword and flail about him, and as he did, a group of about twenty country folk came along the road on their way home

from a fair. The criminals fled, and the travellers crowded round to see the remains of the wife. The body was wrapped up and taken to the magistrates of Glasgow. The case was so sinister that it was reported to the King himself.

The next part of the story, which may be fanciful, is that when the King heard the background to the murder, he personally led a band of four hundred men to Ayrshire to seize the killers. Luckily, they took dogs with them, or they might never have found anything. Some of the dogs set up a furious barking at a

Left: Dr Robert Knox, 1791-1862, Keeper of the Anatomy Museum in Edinburgh and recipient of Burke's and Hare's victims.

little hole in the rocks, and the searchers investigated and discovered the cave.

Inside was a spectacle that beggared description. There were the Beanes, who had now grown to the number of over forty, presumably by incestuous breeding. And a hideous sight they were, but not so hideous as the background.

Legs, arms, feet of men, women and children were hung on the walls in rows, like dried beef. Many limbs lay in pickle, and the cave was scattered with jewellery, pistols, coins and clothes. A count of the family revealed eight Beane sons, six daughters, eighteen grandsons and fourteen granddaughters. The booty and the tribe were haled to Edinburgh.

Under an ancient law concerning red-handed murderers, no trial was necessary. There was a gruesome mass execution, at which the male Beanes had various parts of their bodies amputated and burned before their eyes. Then their arms and legs were cut off and they were left to bleed to death. The females, after witnessing this macabre spectacle, were burned to death. They all died in savage anger, without a trace of repentance.

The foremost historian of Scottish crime, William Roughead, has opined that the Sawney Beane case may be legend, but that too is difficult to prove.

There is no doubt about the harrowing case of Burke and Hare, who are commonly thought of as body-snatchers, but were not. In their time, the early nineteenth century, there was certainly a trade in body-snatching, or Resurrectionism, as it was called. Teachers and students of medicine needed human bodies for the study of anatomy, but the law imposed stringent restrictions on the supply of corpses.

Earlier laws permitted them to take possession of bodies of people who died in the correction house, dead foundlings, suicides and condemned criminals. With the expansion of medical schools, the demand still increased, and the resurrectionists simply robbed fresh graves to supply the anatomists, for cash.

Burke and Hare did sell one body already dead. William Hare was the husband of a lodging-house keeper in Edinburgh, where the lodgers included a fellow Irishman, William Burke and his mistress Helen McDougal. When another elderly lodger died, owing money to Hare, they took the body from its coffin, replaced it with weights, and delivered the corpse to the great anatomist Doctor Robert Knox, who paid £10 for it.

From then on, they did not wait for people to die. Another old man in the lodging house fell ill, and they smothered him with a pillow. They did the same to a young Englishman who contracted jaundice. In another case they lured an elderly woman into the lodging house and murdered her. There were certainly other victims unidentified at the trial.

But the known list was long. One was Mary Paterson, an eighteen-year-old of immoral character but great beauty, who was led into a bout of drinking, with her friend Janet Brown, and taken to the home of Burke's brother, Constantine. She fell unconscious, there was a quarrel, and Janet Brown left, thus saving her own life. At the medical school, one of the students actually recognised the dead girl.

Above: A fairly common sight in older Scottish graveyards, a tomb protected against the resurrectionists. This example is at Greyfriars in Edinburgh.

Below: Daft Jamie, one of the unfortunate victims of Burke and Hare.

Other murders followed, including the particularly brutal killing of an old woman and her grandson, and that of Daft Jamie, a harmless retarded youth familiar in the streets of the city. At one stage there was some animosity among the team, and Mrs Hare actually proposed that they should murder Burke's mistress Helen McDougal. Burke considered that this was going too far, and the couples parted company but they were soon reconciled and back to business. Although Helen McDougal had survived, a relative, Anne McDougal, visited Edinburgh and was smothered to death.

The record of the callous team was certainly well over a dozen murders in barely nine months, and the end of their career came not through brilliant detective work, but drunken stupidity. At Hallowe'en in 1828 there was a rowdy party in the lodging house, and around midnight somebody heard the cry, 'Murder!'

One of the guests noticed that a Mrs Docherty, an old pauper woman, was missing. Nobody could say where she had gone, but another reveller, a Mrs Gray, started to look for her stockings under a bed and saw the body of the old woman there. The criminals tried to bribe her, they threatened her, but she and her husband got away to the authorities. The partnership was ended.

Retribution was less than total. There was a serious lack of evidence, and the authorities decided to prosecute on the Docherty case alone, with Hare as a witness for the prosecution against Burke and McDougal only. The jury at the High Court of Justiciary in Edinburgh, were presented with such a thin case that they brought only a majority against Burke, and refused to find McDougal guilty.

A dark postscript to the case is the judge's remark to Burke on passing the death sentence. 'If it is ever customary to preserve skeletons, yours will be preserved, in order that posterity may keep in remembrance your atrocious crimes.' The skeleton is still in the Anatomical Museum of the University of Edinburgh.

Death did not come into the career of William Brodie, except his own; but there is something very powerful, even gnomic, about the life of a man who lived two lives, one virtuous and one criminal, and probably all for the lust for danger.

Brodie's adventures were also set in Edinburgh, where he was born in the late eighteenth century. He became a cabinet-maker, an honourable calling, he prospered, he inherited £10,000 at the age of twenty-one. He was a Burgess of the city, and a Deacon, which meant that he sat as a judge. But privately, he had expensive tastes.

He maintained a respectable home in Edinburgh, and two others, one for a girl called Anne Grant, the other for Jean Watt and their illegitimate child. He was also a cockfighting enthusiast and an incurable gambler. His extravagances constantly needed more money.

So this charming, capable young man decided to become a criminal. One of his first beautifully simple ideas was inspired by the fact that Edinburgh merchants habitually hung their keys on the inside of their doors during business hours. The Deacon would call on such people and, given a moment when they were not looking, take impressions of the keys with a piece of putty.

It was easy for Brodie to stroll the streets of the capital by night. He was known, he was a top-class citizen, policemen (and there were few of them) would salute him with respect. His depredations were on a big scale, so big that the merchants of the city offered a reward for information leading to the capture of the thief. It was useless. Brodie went blithely on, being respectable and even sternly moral by day, and enjoying his other profession by night.

He took a serious risk when he recruited assistants, two petty criminals and a locksmith, but the success continued, including the theft of the silver mace from Edinburgh University. By day, at the time, he was serving on the jury in a murder case.

However, during an attempt on the Excise office, he was disturbed by an official who had come back late to check on something. The Deacon bowed his head and rushed out, leaving his assistants to fend for themselves and going to Jean Watt's house to establish an alibi.

His friends escaped too. But one of the criminals, John Brown, took fright and decided that his safest course was to inform on his companions, collect the £150 reward and be pardoned. The two others, Andrew Ainslie and George Smith, were arrested.

Now Deacon Brodie was seriously alarmed. He tried to use his office to visit the arrested men, but was refused. Convinced that they would betray him, he fled the city, and immediately came under suspicion. He travelled under an alias and boarded a little boat for France, along with two other passengers, a married couple. They were so amiable that he gave them three letters to post to Scotland when they returned to Britain, and he left the boat at Ostend.

The letters were a mistake. They led to a hue and cry and his arrest in Amsterdam. And in those days, the penal code enjoined the death penalty for almost any crime in the book. He accepted the death sentence, from the infamous Lord Braxfield, with his usual suavity. There is a story that he had arranged for the hangman to be bribed to botch the execution so that he could be rushed away to be resuscitated. Indeed the hanging was a clumsy affair, and he was taken away immediately for private burial. But he was certainly dead.

Doctor Pritchard also had something of the Deacon's histrionic talent. He had enormous charm, and regularly gave public lectures about his travels. They were immensely popular and mostly imaginary. He had pictures of himself made and sold them through newsagents.

He was happily married, with a pleasant house in the West End of Glasgow, and everything was fine for him. There was an unfortunate incident one morning in 1863 when fire broke out in his house, and a servant girl in an upstairs room was killed. But such accidents could happen to any house.

More important, his wife, Mary, who was from Edinburgh, was unhappy and unwell in Glasgow, had regular headaches and bouts of sickness. She proposed to go back to her mother's house in Edinburgh for a rest, and the doctor made the astonishing proposal that she might, if her mother came to Glasgow to take care of him in her absence. His mother-in-law, Mrs Taylor, astonishingly agreed.

The result was that Mrs Pritchard, in Edinburgh, recovered, while Mrs Taylor, in Glasgow, fell ill. Mrs Pritchard was so concerned that she travelled to Glasgow to tend her mother, and soon became ill again herself.

The concerned husband summoned another doctor, Paterson, to see the patients, but first told him privately that the older woman was addicted to a patent medicine containing opium, and was suffering from the effects. Dr Paterson's visit did not help. Mrs Taylor soon died.

When her husband hurried from Edinburgh at the news, the good doctor sent him to Dr Paterson for a death certificate, which was refused. He wrote one himself.

He then went on a visit to Edinburgh, presumably to be away from the scene of unhappy memories, and Dr Paterson called on Mrs Pritchard, to find her so ill that he could do nothing for her, and she too died. It was an anonymous letter that led to Pritchard's arrest, and it is conceivable that it was sent by Dr Paterson, anxious to see justice done but not to be involved.

Pritchard, who loved respectful audiences, had the largest of his life when he was publicly hanged, the last person to be so, on Glasgow Green in 1865.

Left: Deacon Brodie. On the table behind him are keys representing the method of many of his crimes and cards for the gambling habit which was part of the cause of his downfall.

The West End of Glasgow has known another, even more celebrated, violent death. The
scene was Number 7 Blythswood Square, the
home, in the 1880s, of a successful Glasgow
architect, and his family, including his
daughter, Madeleine Smith. Her father was
responsible for the design of the city's McLel-
lan Galleries, which still grace Sauchiehall
Street.

The young Madeleine in 1885 made the
acquaintance of Pierre Emil L'Angelier, a
Channel Islander, and fell madly in love with
him. It was clearly a hopeless passion, since her
father had a position to maintain and the
young man was desperately poor; facts which
made their liaison absolutely obsessional.
Madeleine had an older friend and confidante,
Mary Perry, who made it easy for them to meet,
and they did.

These meetings were not enough, they
longed to be together constantly, and Pierre
regularly came to Blythswood Square to crouch
at the barred window of the basement and
exchange passionate vows with his beloved.

This went on for a year, until Madeleine met
another young man, William Minnoch, a
neighbour of the family who was well established in life and much more the kind of match
of which her family would approve. Minnoch
was tremendously attracted by the beautiful
girl, and she found that she was getting to like
him too. Somehow the dangerous delights of
her secret encounters with Pierre began to pall,
and she finally agreed to marry Minnoch.

She did not quite have the heart to tell Pierre,
or to break it off, and he maintained his visits to
the basement window, and would take cups of
cocoa from Madeleine's hand. After one of
these encounters he was agonisingly sick.

A few days later, it was established, Madeleine bought arsenic, to take to the gardener at
the family's coastal house at Rhu; and that
evening L'Angelier was sick and in agony
again.

A few days later, in the small hours of the
morning, L'Angelier's landlady found him
crouched outside the door, in terrible pain, and
she summoned Mary Perry. But he was dead
before Miss Perry arrived.

Miss Smith's trial at the High Court in
Edinburgh was a national sensation, and there
was competition for places on the public
benches. A key piece of evidence, which might
have been damning, was the letter found on
L'Angelier's body. It was signed Mimi, the
name Madeleine adopted in their correspond-
ence, it was uninhibited and expressed her
blazing desire to see him. And Miss Perry, who
had turned against Madeleine, gave the court
her opinion that the victim must certainly have
responded to the plea on the evening of his
death. The Smith family had also turned away
from the wayward child, and she was alone in
the world.

Left: Dr Pritchard, the last person
to be publicly hanged in
Scotland.

Not entirely alone. She was young, she was
beautiful, she sat through the days of the trial
wonderfully calm, she was the centre of attraction throughout Scotland, and dozens of men
wrote passionate proposals of marriage to her.
She was silent throughout the case, not from
choice, but because of a curious element in
Scottish law which ordained that the accused
person, or 'panel' should sit in the dock without being questioned or making any statement
except the plea of Not Guilty.

Faced with this sweet young lady of striking
beauty and good breeding, the jury was clearly
confused. There were two charges of attempted
murder and one of murder. Their verdict on the
first was Not Guilty, and on the two others Not
Proven, that other quirky feature of Scottish
criminal law which means that while the jury
has strong suspicions, it finds the evidence
inadequate.

In any case, it meant freedom. It also allowed
later students of the case to indulge in all kinds
of speculation; suicide, for instance, which
seems improbable. Even if L'Angelier had
been convinced that the affair was over, and
had chosen to take his own life in despair,
arsenic would have been a hideous choice. And
it was proved that Madeleine had indeed
bought arsenic. Other people have wondered if
the shadowy Mary Perry had been infatuated
with the young Channel Islander and killed
him out of insane jealousy. Too little is known
about the lady to provide grounds for such a
theory.

Madeleine survived the ordeal, removed
herself from her hostile family and moved to
London, where she married, and for a while
was the charming centre of an intellectual
radical clique. Later she emigrated to New York

Right: The American artist
Whistler's portrait of *Thomas
Carlyle*, reminiscent of Whistler's
more famous study of his mother.
Thomas Carlyle, 1795-1881, born
in Ecclefechan, was regarded by
his contemporaries as among the
most important literary figures of
his day. His best known work is
probably his massive history of
the French Revolution.

and had no difficulty in finding other friends. She lived very happily, as far as can be deduced, until over ninety.

In the old-fashioned dance the Paul Jones, the music periodically stops and everybody has to change partners. John Paul Jones was the Scot who certainly switched his allegiance, and gave Scotland some painful experiences. Born John Paul, son of a gardener in Kirkcudbright-shire, he went to sea as a boy and saw America several times. He served for several years on a slave-ship without, as far as is known, feeling any compunction for his grim trade, and when he inherited a piece of property in America at the age of twenty-six, he left the sea and made his home in Virginia, but when America decided to found a navy he got involved in the preparations and the outbreak of the Revolutionary War gave him his real trade as a devil-may-care adventurer.

In 1778, in command of an American brig, he penetrated the Solway Firth to harry his former compatriots by setting one British ship on fire, spiking 36 guns, and making off with a Scottish nobleman's family silver. (When the war was over he returned it, to show that he too had some nobility.) His capture of the British sloop *Drake* off Ireland is the first recorded American naval triumph. He attacked the port of Leith at the head of a French squadron flying American colours; and captured two men-of-war off Flamborough Head. He was invincible.

He joined the Russian Navy in 1788 to fight against Turkey. He was a fully formed legend when he died in Paris, honoured by the U.S. Congress and ennobled by Louis XVI of France. He was only 45, but it was a crowded lifetime.

James Young Simpson brought gentleness into the stern and often brutal world of the mid nineteenth century. When he was appointed professor of midwifery at Edinburgh Royal Infirmary, he used ether to numb the pains of childbirth, and it took courage. The Bible had said that women would labour in pain to bring forth children, and the medical profession of the time took that not as a statement of fact, but as a divine order, which it would be sacrilegious to defy or evade. The medical profession was exclusively male.

Simpson did not invent chloroform, but his experiments showed him that in a refined form it was the anaesthetic he had been looking for. There was powerful opposition among doctors and clerics, and it was not until 1853 that he triumphed, when he administered it to Queen Victoria during the birth of Prince Leopold. What was good for the Queen was clearly good for everybody, and the Queen trusted him completely, having appointed him her physician in Scotland. He made other advances in the medical practices of his time, but is rightly remembered for this victory. He did not merely bring a scientific advance into medicine. He brought compassion.

Modern people smile at Samuel Smiles, but this was a Scotsman who took life very seriously, believed in the innate goodness of mankind, and did what he could to bring it out. He qualified in medicine at the age of twenty,

Above: Sir Walter Scott's mansion at Abbotsford.

Above: Sir James Young Simpson, 1811-70, pioneer in the use of chloroform.

Above right: Samuel Smiles, 1812-1904, moralist and social reformer.

and practised in Edinburgh and Leeds, but turned to journalism and later to executive work on the railways. He had started writing in his twenties, and produced a long list of books including a life of George Stephenson, the railway pioneer, but his best-seller was *Self-Help*, a marvellously Victorian work of rugged moralising aimed at children, who were invited to read the brief biographies of great men and exhorted to rise to equal eminence by their own efforts. It was the favourite school prize of Victorian times, at least among the teachers who chose it, and was prodigiously successful in America too. It was republished as recently as 1986.

The conventional reputation of Allan Pinkerton is that his great detective agency never slept, and that it solved crimes baffling to the regular police forces. Such coups were not really the stuff of his career, which was largely devoted to working for the American railroads against labour organisations and strikers. It is ironic that Pinkerton fled from his native Glasgow because he was involved in the Chartist movement when the British Government was taking direct action against such subversives and their call for universal franchise and annual Parliamentary elections.

He was trained as a cooper, and when he reached Dundee in Illinois in 1842 he took up the trade there, but dreamed of better things, like making crime pay a detective. In the unsophisticated context of his time some of his ingenious tricks attracted admiration, such as

hiding inside a barrel to listen to secret discussions, and keeping an eye open for camp fires when in pursuit of suspects in the dark. He became deputy sheriff, later joined the secret service, and had the duty of guarding President Lincoln – some years before the assassination, it must be said. He rose to head of the secret service before he founded the first private eye organisation, centred in Chicago. Quite early in the agency's existence, there arose a working-class song called *My Father was killed by a Pinkerton Man*. And that is how the agency was seen by the labour movement in America. But the legend lives on.

John Alexander Macdonald was the son of an unemployed engineer in the Townhead district of Glasgow, and the possibility is that if he had stayed there, he would have grown up to be an unemployed engineer. Instead, he created the Dominion of Canada.

John A. Macdonald emigrated as a boy to Kingston, in what was then Upper Canada, and studied and worked hard to become a successful lawyer before he became active in politics. The provinces of Upper and Lower Canada (Quebec) united in 1841, and three years later he was elected to Parliament as a moderate Conservative, rising to cabinet rank a few years later. Macdonald was a great compromiser, in the best sense of being able to persuade opposing camps to compromise with each other, and he created the alliance of the English-speaking Conservatives and the French Liberals.

The parliament of the united provinces had early troubles because each had equal representation and no government could get a commanding majority of any duration. It was Macdonald who pushed for a new federal constitution, enshrined in the British North America Act and creating the federation of Ontario, Quebec, Nova Scotia and New Brunswick. Macdonald was its first Prime Minister. He organised the purchase of what are now the Prairie Provinces from the Hudson Bay Company, and in 1870 Prince Edward Island and British Columbia joined a Dominion that stretched from ocean to ocean.

His career dipped badly in a scandal involving the transcontinental railroad which had been promised to British Columbia to induce it to join, and there were charges that Macdonald's party had been given huge funds by the railroad construction company. But he was back in power in 1878, and the railway did go through a few years later.

John A. Macdonald is truly the father of the Dominion. A cheerful, outgoing man of great charm, he certainly had his dark private depressions. His wife died young, and his first child, and he had few close friends. But all in all he was a great Canadian. It is not surprising that he drank, sometimes too much and with

Left: Robert Louis Stevenson, 1850-94, painted here by Count Giralamo Nerli, is best remembered for his brilliant adventure stories like *Treasure Island*, but also produced other notable works on more serious themes.

Below: Allan Pinkerton (left), seen during his time as an intelligence chief with President Lincoln (centre) during the American Civil War.

Left: Mary Slessor, seated, with some of the twins whom she saved.

visible and audible symptoms. But it is recorded that on one occasion when he was in full and slightly fuddled flight in the Chamber, a member remarked to his neighbour that he would rather listen to John A. Macdonald drunk than any other man sober.

In 1956, Queen Elizabeth laid a wreath on a grave at Mission Hill in Calabar. It was a tribute to the undiminished memory of a Dundee girl who gave most of her life to teaching and caring for Africans in what is now Nigeria. Mary Slessor came naturally to caring for other people. Her father was an amiable drunkard and no provider, and when she was hardly into her teens she was working in a Dundee jute mill and helping to look after her younger brothers and sisters.

She was also a Sunday school teacher and a social missionary in a city which in the 1860s needed a lot of social work. It was a city also fascinated by Africa, and the young Mary was enthralled by visiting missionaries from Calabar. She was tough and resilient and even hoydenish, quite happy to be nicknamed Carrots and afraid of nobody. She merely envied her older brother John's preparations to follow those missionaries to Calabar, the White Man's Grave, riddled with malaria, blackwater fever and yellow fever. When John died she applied for his place.

Scantily educated, she turned out to be a facile linguist and learned the local Efik language during training before she left for Africa. She was twenty-eight, and in Africa she was equally happy to be known as Big Ma,

teaching and preaching, training women in domestic science and dispensing medicines and herbal cures, first at Duke Town and then

Left: Charles Rennie Mackintosh, 1869-1928, architect and designer, and early pioneer of the Art Nouveau style, by Francis Henry Newbery.

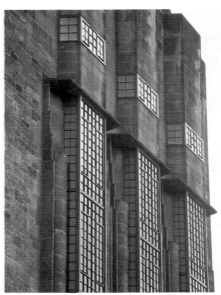

Above: Mackintosh's ideas on design embraced every household item, decorations and furniture, as well as the basic architecture.

Above right: One of the façades of the Glasgow School of Art, one of Mackintosh's most successful and highly regarded designs.

Below right: Hugh MacDiarmid by William Menzies. MacDiarmid was perhaps the finest Scottish poet of modern times. Much of his most important work is written in Scots and deals with nationalistic themes.

Below: Sir Harry Lauder, 1870-1950, comedian and singer, in a painting by H M Bateman, made a career of exploiting, with great charm, the sort of tartan sentimentality which MacDiarmid despised.

in inland towns. One of her long-standing campaigns was against the local belief that if girl twins were born, one came from a good spirit and the other from an evil spirit. The unwanted twin was sometimes quietly killed, sometimes abandoned to die. The mission rescued and reared unwanted twins, and when Mary was sent home on sick leave she took a little adopted girl, Janice, with her – both from love and from the urge to show off the child to raise enthusiasm for the missionary cause.

When she went back to Africa she was intermittently ill for the rest of her life, but she worked on, totally uninterested in her own welfare, and spread sweetness and light till her death in 1915.

Another Scot who made the world a smaller place, and who cared, was Alexander Graham Bell. His father, Alexander Melville Bell, was a teacher and student of phonetics, and he in-

vented a device to produce 'visible sound', an optical analogue of human speech. The son, also born in Edinburgh carried on the work, particularly in its application to the deaf, and like James Young Simpson, he sometimes found himself in a hostile environment, in a time when the deaf were sometimes regarded as mentally defective, to be hidden away. Bell was determined to help them to communicate, and he did.

America is probably entitled to claim him, since he moved to Canada for his health and later settled in Boston, and it was there that he applied his studies to the production of the first magnetic telephone. His contribution to society speaks for itself.

And where Bell let us speak from afar, John Logie Baird let us see. He was not the only man seeking for the means of sending pictures. The Russian Nipkov had already invented a disc,

with a spiral line of tiny holes, which could do the trick in a rudimentary fashion. It was revolved against another disc with a small square hole, and the little holes transmitted a changing pattern of light and shade reflected from a solid object. This could be reproduced by another disc synchronised with the first.

It was an interesting toy. Logie Baird worked obsessionally, usually in poverty, to transform it. By 1926 he had perfected a 30-line television process. It was taken up by the British Broadcasting Corporation as an experiment, and developed into a 240-line system. The process had the limitation of depending on mechanical scanning, and it was soon to be pushed aside by the immensely more flexible electronic process. But Baird had laid the ground, and before he died in 1946 he had produced colour and three-dimensional TV.

Robert Watson Watt gave the world artificial eyes too. In 1935, when it had been officially decided that there was no possibility of using radiated beams in air warfare, he produced a completely developed system which he called radiolocation. Watson Watt acknowledged his debt to Marconi, who had done some inconclu-

sive experiments in the field a decade before. Some work had been tried in Germany, but the German government had dismissed it. With Watson Watt, it was a vision that worked.

Alexander Fleming's discovery of penicillin

Above: Lord Kelvin's last lecture, 1899.

Below: John Logie Baird at work on an early television.

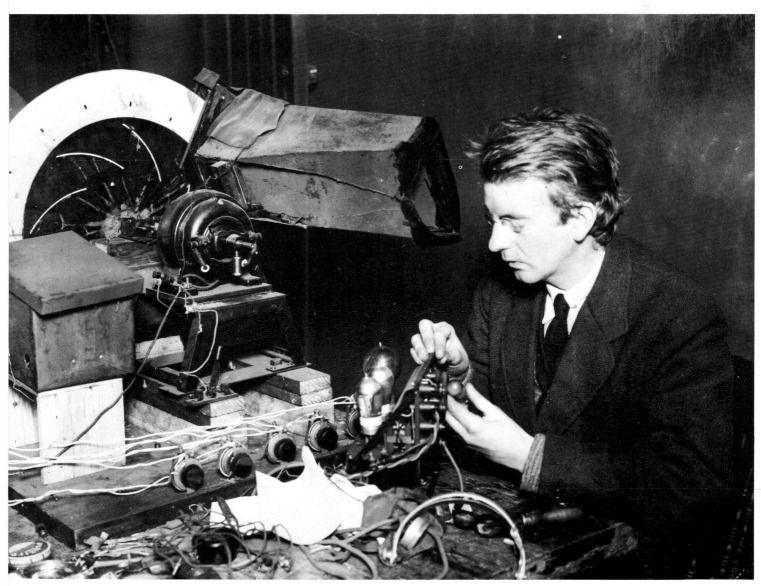

Left: Sir Arthur Conan Doyle.

was an interesting accident. Working in his laboratory in 1928, he noticed a mound of mould on a plate reserved for a culture of bacteria, and became interested in its effects. It destroyed some bacterial species and not others, which was a valuable discovery in itself, because the mould could be used to separate some species from others.

Other people became involved, because Fleming could not isolate the essential element. Florey and Chain, at Oxford succeeded in finding the significant ingredient, which Fleming had failed to do. In World War II, the United States, with immensely superior resources, was able to produce the material on a huge scale, and it saved lives on a huge scale.

If Scotland produced the first famous private detective, it threw up a keener mind in the creator of the first fictitious private detective. Arthur Conan Doyle turned to writing because he was not making much money as a doctor, and produced the character of Sherlock Holmes, who applied pure reason to mysterious crimes. Holmes first appeared in the *Strand* Magazine in 1891, and became so celebrated that the author, who would rather have been writing historical novels, tried to kill him off, but was overwhelmed by the enthusiasm of his readers and had to arrange a resurrection.

Holmes was the first. The emulators are numbered in thousands. Conan Doyle created an entire new form of literary art.

8 Homes and Schools

ONE OF THE most massive tasks facing Scotland in modern times, and less-than-modern times, was the simple one of housing the people in the expanding cities. Even before the Industrial Revolution, eighteenth century Edinburgh had acquired a dense congestion of slum tenements, some over ten storeys high, and the life of the poor was squalid, diseased and usually short.

There is an old Scottish dance tune, *The Floo'ers o' Edinburgh*, which sounds pretty but whose title is a cynical recollection of that squalor. Hygiene and sanitation in those areas did not exist. Householders disposed of waste, including human waste, by throwing it from an open window into the street, with the warning shout, 'Gardeyloo,' from the French *gardez*

l'eau, look out for the water. The neglected filth in the streets was what was meant by the flowers of Edinburgh.

But the massive congestion of the cities came with the Industrial Revolution, and Victorian Scotland was a welter of city slums, and Victorian Glasgow provided the clearest and worst examples.

Until that time, the typical working-class home in the city was a tenement of two or three storeys, often with outside staircases to the upper flats, very much like working-class houses to be found in rustic villages. The city, starting as a fishing village running from the Cathedral down to the river, first spread out to the east, and as late as the nineteenth century the area to the west and to the south of the river was a pastoral community.

Previous page: The *Low Green* in Glasgow in 1808 as painted by J Brooks.

Left: Fruit Seller by Walter Geikie, 1795-1837, an Edinburgh artist who specialised in scenes of his native city and of country affairs.

The pressure on population came both with industry and with the displacement of country people from the Highlands and later from Ireland. The Irish peasantry lived on a staple diet of potatoes, and in the 1840s – the Hungry Forties – a mysterious blight wiped out the crops. Emigration and death from starvation reduced the population by millions, and there was a mass movement to the nearest British towns and cities, Liverpool and the Clyde.

The influx of these strangers, from the North and from across the Irish Sea, shaped the character of the Glaswegian, a powerful blend of the new invaders – tall, blond and redhaired Highlanders, dark-haired Highlanders, dark Irish and the original Scottish Lowlander descended from Pictish strains. The Picts were small and dark with long heads, and the type can still be seen in the city at any football match.

The city that greeted the incomers, often with suspicion of their strange manners and their foreign tongues, was soon in the throes of a dramatic expansion, and its housing development was designed to cram the maximum number of families into the least possible area. The new form of dwelling was the Glasgow tenement, and many of them have survived.

Tenement buildings are usually three or four storeys high, with each block built as a hollow rectangle enclosing an open space. On the ground floor, entries known as closes lead from the street outside to the court behind, and a stone staircase leads off the middle of the close to the landings above.

Tenements varied widely in quality and amenity. All had running cold water. A small proportion had baths. Some had indoor toilets. In many, the families on each landing shared a toilet. In the more spacious, and expensive, there were two, or three, family houses on each landing; but four and more houses per landing were common. There was a wide distribution of houses containing a kitchen and one other room, and an enormous number consisting of nothing but a kitchen, 'single ends' as they were known. (The word 'end' used to mean a room, can still be heard in Glasgow.) The standard sleeping arrangement was the set-in bed, an alcove in the wall accommodating a mattress, and the standard length of the mattress was 4 feet 8 inches or 1.4 metres. Most kitchens had two, some more.

And into these tiny apartments came the new industrial working classes, to live and increase. Families of ten or fifteen were commonplace, and death was commonplace too.

The mechanism of infection was not yet understood. There was a general feeling, in fact, that overcrowding made life cosier. Typhus was endemic in the cities, and there were periodic outbreaks of cholera and smallpox. One child in twenty died in infancy.

The tenements were good business, and the more congested the better. When prosperous people abandoned their good-quality tene-

ment flats to move elsewhere, the flats were subdivided to squeeze in the poor and raise the profits; and intensify the squalor and the disease. Another scourge that soon established itself was tuberculosis, which regularly wiped out entire families, and remained an important problem in Scotland until the 1950s.

The tenement-dwellers accepted their lot with little complaint, since it was the only lot they knew. And although industry made huge fortunes, wages were kept low, almost as a matter of moral principle, on the basis that if the lower classes had more money they would spend it on drink.

And drink, certainly, was another curse of Scotland. In the middle of the nineteenth century it was reported that there was one public house to every fourteen families. But it could be claimed that drink, and producing children, were the only relaxations available to the poor of the cities. Dundee weavers were paid ten shillings a week or less, they started work at half past five in the morning and worked till seven in the evening. And not only grown men, but boys and girls under fourteen years of age. Drink was cheap, and it brought its own social troubles including alcohol-related disease.

The population growth was explosive. In the first thirty years of the nineteenth century, Glasgow's population rose from 77,000 to 200,000. Within a further century it expanded five-fold. Dundee's population increased in the same thirty years from 27,000 to over 45,000.

Dundee was too small to contain this expansion, and had to extend its boundaries; but not into bright new suburbs, rather endless rows of dreary tenements built without regard to health or beauty, without drains or an efficient water supply. Most of the individual homes were of one or two rooms, and the health hazards of the old inner city were perpetuated.

Aberdeen, with a tradition of building in durable granite, coped relatively well with its population increase. The capital city of Edinburgh was no better than Glasgow or Dundee.

The very word tenement acquired ugly overtones; but some of the more prosperous citizens of all four cities were very happy with the pattern because it could provide grace and space for those who could afford it. When Glasgow, for instance, began to expand westward around the middle of the nineteenth century, it was into some terraced houses of great elegance, but also into tenements of high quality, with individual homes of four, five or more spacious rooms, with bathrooms and hot water systems. They have survived to the present day as highly desirable residences.

The crowded working-class houses had one accidental advantage, which has been mourned by many Scots who finally were able to move away from the congestion. They induced a feeling of community which was peculiar to them. Families living in the same

Left: Gladstone's Land is the best surviving example of the sort of tall tenement which formerly was common in Edinburgh's Old Town. The six-storey house is now owned by the National Trust for Scotland.

close had privacy when they closed their doors, but they all knew one another and could depend on one another in the mundane troubles of life, from illness or accident to being short of a spoonful of tea.

The children too were under a protective cover of neighbourliness. A small child playing in the back court was visible not only from his own kitchen window but from all the kitchen windows; and if he found himself in trouble, three or four housewives at their kitchen sinks, who knew him, could see the trouble and be ready to help. If some youngster from another street arrived to bully him, for instance, the stranger was immediately identified as a stranger, and driven off.

Below: In contrast with Gladstone's Land illustrated above is the Georgian House in Charlotte Square owned by the National Trust for Scotland and representative of the style of Edinburgh's New Town. The building was designed by Robert Adam.

Above: Tickets from Glasgow ticketed houses. Top, in tin dating from 1866 and, above, in cast iron from 1900.

Left: A charming portrait by an unknown artist of a woman shopkeeper in Glasgow in the 1790s.

So, by an odd chance, petty crime was held in check. Aside from drunken brawls, the squalid tenement areas were law-abiding places. In terms of modern criminology, the strongest force towards law and order is not the police, but public opinion and people's knowledge of their neighbours. This was to be proved by later, idealistic developments in working-class housing.

There was nothing idealistic in the building of the old houses. They were simply a business investment, and very successful as businesses. And there was no control of rents, which were simply determined by market forces. This was demonstrated by the 1915 rent strike in Glasgow, a protest against rent increases, and for the first time the Government intervened with restrictive laws.

It was not until after the Great War that housing began to be seen as a public responsibility as well as a business, and the civic authorities were able to get finance from a Public Works Loan Board to build houses for rent. The rents in many cases were subsidised by the city councils to bring them within the range of working-class tenants.

Oddly enough, in Glasgow for instance, there was a three-tier system of building. At the bottom were tenements of respectable amenities called Slum Clearance, to house families regarded as on the bottom social rung. Other tenements were called Intermediate. At the top were pleasant little cottages each of four

family flats, terraces and semi-detached villas, all with gardens, built on farm land on the city fringes. For the relatively few families whose names came up on the long waiting lists, they were the realisation of a dream.

The demand for such homes was so strong that some householders were willing to pay for a better place on the waiting lists, and there were instances of bribery, some of them discovered, of officials and city councillors. But generally, the new housing policy brought a new and healthy style of life to many ordinary

Below: The kitchen in the Georgian House in Edinburgh's Charlotte Square is furnished as it might have been by the first owners.

people, and construction went on into the early thirties.

The shortage of homes was still a huge social problem. After World War II, it was estimated that Glasgow had a deficit of over 100,000 houses. The inner city still had blocks of old tenements whose doors carried a metal plate with the mysterious inscription '2½', put there by the public health authority to indicate that the maximum permitted size of the family inside was two adults and one child. In such flats, an occupant could literally lie in the 'box bed', reach over and open the door to a visitor.

The housing problem was still seen as primarily a responsibility of the local authorities, and when materials and labour became available after the wartime shortages, huge housing projects were set in motion. Their size was governed by urgent need, but it also demonstrated what one critic of planning (the author) called the Arithmetical Heresy.

Pre-war housing schemes had individually been fairly small groups of a few hundred homes, in which some of the old neighbourly atmosphere of the tenements was able to thrive. People knew their immediate neighbours well, and their more distant neighbours by sight. The Arithmetical Heresy was the idea that if a neighbourhood of 500 homes was good, a neighbourhood of 10,000 homes would be twenty times better. This was soon seen to be less than completely true.

The idealistic political urge was to provide houses for the homeless, and forget for the moment the other things that contribute to a neighbourhood: libraries, swimming baths, shops, cafes and meeting places. Public houses would never be considered. Glasgow City Council, regarding drink as a curse, had a rule that it would not be involved in the trade by permitting alcohol to be sold on land that it owned.

One large scheme on the south side of the city had a population larger than the City of Perth, with few shops, not a single cafe and of course, no public houses. One simple result was that men who still insisted on drink had to make long bus journeys towards the city to find a bar, and very often had many drinks in a hurry to justify the trip. Buses back to those suburbs after closing time were full of noise and unpleasantness.

And unlike the older, smaller housing projects, these enormous schemes had difficulty in generating a sense of neighbourhood. Far from being recognisable to neighbours, people, and especially young people, found themselves anonymous. It is an unpleasant feeling. It also makes it easier to indulge in petty crime without being identified, and the response was seen in regular vandalism.

In the Craigmillar estate in Edinburgh, largely a tenemental growth, social conditions deteriorated so badly that many residents

Above: Tightly packed tenements in Victorian Glasgow. This picture was taken just off Glasgow's High Street in the 1860s.

Left: Inside a tenement in Glasgow's Gorbals district in 1948. In the background is the box bed in the alcove which was a standard feature of most tenement houses.

Above right: Occupants of a Dundee tenement enjoy a sunny afternoon on the 'plettie.' This type of design was most common in the Dundee area.

Right: Briefly the pride and joy of Glasgow's Housing Department, the Red Road Flats.

simply left and other prospective tenants refused to move in. Entire blocks had their windows boarded up to protect the empty houses from vandalism, and there, as in one part of Glasgow, residents first saw the unexpected spectacle of shops with steel shutters on the windows.

The local authorities, with good intentions, had found a solution that contained a new problem. When they looked for a new solution, the development of the tower crane in the sixties offered it. In Dundee and Glasgow, the Arithmetical Heresy was adopted again: if people had been happy in three-storey tenements, they would be ten times happier in thirty storeys.

The Dundee response to the new technology was to destroy much of the heart of the city and cover the suburban landscape with rows of high-rise blocks of flats. Identical towers rose on sites in Glasgow, where the ancient district of Gorbals was demolished to make room for the new pattern. On another Glasgow site, to the north, the city proposed, and built with pride, what were to be the highest housing blocks in Europe, the Red Road Flats.

The solution soon began to display its own problems. It was not possible for residents to generate neighbourly feelings in buildings where they rarely saw their neighbours except in lifts. Sometimes they failed to get on to lifts because the lifts were already full of strange neighbours. Lacking the finance for security and maintenance available to owner-occupier skyscrapers, the blocks were subject to vandalism, and to lift breakdowns. There were cases of schoolchildren organising teams to run

errands for elderly people trapped in high blocks with lifts out of action. In some blocks, faults in design or construction led to sheets of facing material falling off, with danger to the residents and to passers-by.

An astonishing aspect of the Red Road Flats is that although they of course have staircases as well as lifts, the staircases are accessible only through a bedroom in each flat, so that a visitor who finds himself in the hallway of an upper storey when the lift fails is trapped unless one of the residents on that storey is at home and willing to let him leave through the bedroom. The noble dream of high living, then, turned out to have elements of nightmare.

Around the same time as the arrival of the tower blocks, there was another scheme to reduce the population pressure, particularly in Glasgow, by decanting surplus citizens into completely new towns, which would have all the qualities of neighbourliness together with clean country air and small-town amenity, as

well as attracting new, clean industries to make them self-sufficient.

On the whole, this has succeeded. The first new town, East Kilbride, was built round the pleasant rural village of the same name, but without demolishing it, and became attractive to Glaswegians looking for a new start in a new place. One objection raised to the whole concept was that new towns were likely to attract the young and energetic from the city, and drain some of the city's human energy in the process. This is true in a degree of all emigration.

In the event, a good proportion of the people who moved into the new towns simply regarded them as home bases from which to commute to work in the city. Many of the pioneers found them featureless and un-cosy and anonymous. But as industries developed and the raw look wore off, the new towns have acquired identities and local patriotism, and there is now a rising generation which has never known any other home.

There were, inevitably, mistakes. Cumbernauld, also built beside an old village, is unusually cold and windy in winter because of its altitude. Naturalists, who were not consulted in advance, have pointed out that before

the new buildings covered the landscape, it was one on which no small animal life was found, the dumb creatures regarding it as too high up for a reasonable life. And visitors find the well-preserved little houses in the old village the most attractive homes in the area. But Cumbernauld people are not unhappy with their new ambience.

There is also strong local patriotism in Glenrothes, in Fife, whose site was originally

Above: Typical examples of the most successful new housing built in the 1930s. Such properties are still generally more highly regarded than some modern developments. This picture was taken in Rutherglen, near Glasgow.

Below: A modern success, the new town of Glenrothes.

Above: An example of the refurbishment of old tenements. The stonework on these Glasgow properties has been cleaned and the back courts renovated.

chosen because of the rich coal deposits beneath it, providing a ready-made industry as a base. Unfortunately, it was soon discovered that the position of the coal in relation to water made it impossible to mine. The town has attracted other industries instead.

Irvine was, and still is, a douce little seaside town when the New Town grew around it. Its principal trouble in recent years is one that it shares with other towns new and old, the contraction of industry and the growth of unemployment. The new towns, however, are in no sense a disaster as some other great visions turned out to be.

A fifth new town was planned at Houston, in Renfrewshire, but the concept of new towns had been studied and revised in the light of experience and the plan was abandoned. Nevertheless, Scotland's new towns are there to stay.

Drink has already been mentioned in this chapter, and it is worth expanding on here, since it has to do with cities and towns as well as remote hamlets.

The Scots throughout their history have in general been harder drinkers than their English neighbours. During the period of the Auld Alliance, sophisticated Scots consumed large quantities of claret, and whisky, often home-made, tended to be the drink of the peasantry. When it was commercially produced, it was sold at once to innkeepers, who retailed it within weeks to their customers, at a strength of 70 per cent by volume, compared with today's usual strength of 40 per cent. Until

the nineteenth century, most whisky was sent to England for a further process of distillation and used as the base ingredient for gin.

There is a good deal of mystery and mystique surrounding Scotch whisky, some of it authentic. It is said, convincingly, that two malt whiskies made by the identical process will differ in personality when the water used in the process comes from streams only a hundred yards apart. And although the manufacture is highly mechanised, it still depends on the nose and nous of the stillman in knowing exactly when to discard the early and the late flow and accept only the perfect spirit in the middle of the run.

Most of the whisky drunk today is blended, and this too involves human skill in keeping consistent the flavour of a particular brand year after year. And it is never drunk within weeks of distilling, but left to mature in wood casks for a legal minimum of three years.

The fairly savage raw spirit of older times was the favoured tipple of Scotsmen, and sometimes women, and remained favourite. Spirits, including whisky, are of course drunk in England, but the basic English tradition is a leisurely pint of beer, while the Scots is spirits, hard and fast.

It became more leisurely in 1976, with a change in the law governing public house hours; a change regarded by many people as highly dangerous. The Scots have always been in two minds about drink. One, that it was the best medicine, the other that it was a product of the devil and should be abolished entirely.

Above: A Scotch Fair by Alexander Fraser, 1786-1865, probably painted around 1834, illustrates the vitality of market town life in the period.

The pattern of permitted drinking hours before 1976 in Scotland was from 11 am till 2.30 pm, and from 5 till 10 pm. This was not exactly an ancient tradition. The afternoon closure was introduced, for both England and Scotland, during World War I, under the Defence of the Realm Act, and its motive was to ensure that munitions and other essential workers would be put out of the pubs to return to their benches in the afternoons.

That war ended, but the restriction remained. There were interesting differences, however, between the English and the Scottish situations. Pubs in England opened on Sundays. Pubs in Scotland were compelled to observe the Sabbath. But there was a strange loophole, in the Bona Fide Travellers Act, applying only to Scotland. This recognised that a traveller was entitled to food and drink on his journey, even on a Sunday, and hotels could serve such a traveller from midnight on Saturday until midnight on Sunday.

To a large extent, the Act was a joke. There were occasions on which the drinkers from one Highland village would trek the necessary three miles to a neighbouring village, while

Church of Scotland and other groups. One academic opponent pointed out that when liquor was freely available, people simply drank more of it. France, for instance, where there are no restrictions, has an incidence of liver cirrhosis three times that of Britain. And even during the period of restricted hours, cirrhosis was commoner in Scotland than in England.

The restrictions were removed nevertheless. Ten years later, a survey carried out to report on the results suggested that in general, the relaxation had been beneficial. There were no longer crowds of drunk men staggering in the streets after a frantic bout of drinking before closing time. It also found that more women were using public houses, though it was hard to tell whether this was a result of the relaxation or merely of changes in the general attitude of women, and of society to women.

There had also been a tentative recommendation that some public houses might have rooms where families could sit together, parents and children, but this was too revolutionary for Scottish publicans, and the family rooms did not appear.

Even after ten years, the opposition persisted, partly on the grounds that although drunkenness was no longer as obvious, it was still there, and that apart from visible intoxication, there was an increased long-term absorption of alcohol leading to the alcohol-related diseases, particularly dangerous to women, whose resistance is lower than men's.

It is not easy to say why Scots have a more urgent appetite for drink than their English neighbours. The colder climate may have an influence, the Celtic ancestry too – the Irish Celts also have deep appetites. Insecurity and the urge to appear virile have also been suggested. The sordid history of the Scottish cities since the Industrial Revolution is doubtless also relevant.

By what may be coincidence, the same ten years of relaxation in Glasgow have seen another transformation in that city. Certainly, it has 260 tower housing blocks. But instead of demolishing what remains of the Victorian tenements, the city has carried out a big-scale scheme of renovating them. In some, two small flats have been knocked into one, providing space for bathrooms. And over a great part of the city, the black grime built up by decades of soot-laden air has been cleaned off the facades, showing the original attractive sandstone of cream or pink colour.

And significantly, these improvements were not, on the whole, imposed from above, but initiated by residents themselves, who wanted improvement but also wanted to stay in the tenement streets they enjoyed. The freedom to make that decision is a revolution as notable as the freedom to drink at will, and perhaps a bigger one.

those from the second village trekked in the opposite direction, each group to drink legally for as long as it chose.

A large change came with the report of the Clayson Committee to the Secretary of State for Scotland in 1973, with recommendations that were implemented in 1976. These were that with certain minor provisos, Scottish public houses could apply for permission to open from 11 am until 11 pm, and could also apply for Sunday licences which would, however, incorporate the afternoon closure.

There was powerful opposition, from the

The Scots have a traditional and deep-seated pride in the country's educational system and its history; and the story is certainly impressive. As late as 1855, at marriages in Scotland, 87 per cent of husbands and 77 per cent of wives were able to sign the register. The comparative figures in England were 70 per cent and 59 per cent. A few years later, a survey revealed that one pupil in 205 in Scotland was undertaking higher education. The English figure was one in 1300.

Around the same period, Sir Walter Besant wrote an article for an English periodical containing this passage:

'Do Scotsmen always know that it is their John Knox and all he did for his country, that now wherever the pilgrim turns his feet he finds Scotsmen in the forefront of battle, of civilisation, of art and letters?

'They are premiers in every colony, professors in every university, teachers, editors, lawyers, engineers, merchants, everything – always in the front.

'Education! John Knox saw that want and supplied the need. Freedom of thought, free-

dom of speech, freedom of action. John Knox supplied all these. For a monument, if you want, circumspice – look round the world!'

The story has some truth, but it is not quite so simple. It is clear that the Scots have always had a passionate lust for learning, as have many other peoples, and that they have done something quite important to satisfy it. But history, as another irreverent historian has said, is not what happened, but what we remember. And the history of Scottish education has its downs as well as its ups.

It begins with Saint Columba, that literate, violent man who brought his Christianity to Scotland in the year 563. Religion and literacy were intertwined, and it is only with the evangelical colonisation by Columba's followers that we find the first signs of written language among the native Picts, who certainly had a lively spoken language but had never put pen to paper before Columba, who was based on Iona but ranged widely over Scotland.

It would be a mistake to imagine a rapid creation of universal education. For centuries education flourished in small pockets, invariably adjuncts to churches or abbeys, and was enjoyed by very few Scots. But we find sizeable schools at St Andrews by 1120, at Perth, Dunfermline and Stirling by the middle of the same century and at Aberdeen in 1262; and it is in the thirteenth century that first mention is made of private endowments to help impoverished scholars.

The modern pupil would hardly feel at home if he were transported back in time to one of those schools. Latin was the language of the classroom, and as late as 1494 a priest in Glasgow who tried to give a lesson in the vernacular tongue was sharply censured. And higher learning was simply not available. The Scotsman – and education was a male prerogative – who wanted to go further simply had to go.

Many bright young men packed a knapsack and left the country, for England, for the universities of Paris, Heidelberg, Bologna and elsewhere on the continent. Although education also had a class significance, they were not all wealthy. They would take casual jobs to earn their meagre bread, or even busk in the streets.

Intellectually, they were the equal of any continental scholars. A towering example is Johannes Duns Scotus, born in 1265 in Roxburghshire, who studied at Oxford and was very soon teaching philosophy and theology there. His mastery is indicated by the tale, doubtless exaggerated, that he attracted 30,000 students. At times he also lectured in Paris and Cologne. There is no doubt that the universal use of Latin made it simple for scholars and teachers to take their skills and their ambitions to other countries. Latin was the Esperanto of the academic world.

Duns, a Franciscan, also cheerfully engaged in the theological arguments that were never

Below: John Knox returning home after preaching his last sermon. Although Knox's schemes for universal schooling were never implemented as he would have wished, an important foundation had been laid.

far away in the old church. He took the Realist view, invented it, in fact, and rejected the theoretical approach established by Aristotle in favour of the practical. Faith, he held, was not speculative but practical, an act of will. If the distinction seems too subtle – and he was nicknamed Doctor Subtilis – the controversy has never entirely disappeared, and would rear up later in some sections of the Presbyterian faith disguised as the clash between the doctrine of free will and that of predestination. He unwittingly gave a new word to the language, dunce, from the contemptuous 'Duns man' applied to his followers by the other parties in the dispute.

The entanglement between religion and education was deep and durable. In the early days of the sixteenth century, many Scots clergymen actually believed that Martin Luther had recently composed a wicked book called the New Testament, while they were determined to stick to the Old Testament. And Latin was equally long-lasting. A century later, Latin syntax was actually taught from rules written in Latin, a process that would probably appeal to Joseph Heller, the *Catch-22* author.

And the rod was not spared. In some schools using this convoluted system, a boy was automatically flogged if he could not say the lesson for the day. If he could say it, he was flogged so that he would still remember it a day later.

Some Scots assume that widespread education came to the country with the Reformation, but in fact, St Andrews University was set up as

early as 1411, to be followed by Glasgow in 1451 and Aberdeen in 1495. Of the old universities, only Edinburgh's foundation, in 1583, came after the Reformation. And they were not entirely a blessing. In their early days they were raw, and small, with limited courses and very scant libraries, so that brainy Scots were getting much less out of them than if they had followed the tracks of their predecessors to the richly endowed establishments abroad.

But the nation still threw up its full quota of outstanding academics. George Buchanan, born at Killearn in 1506, went through the parish school rapidly and was studying at the University of Paris by the time he was fifteen. He taught at other European universities before becoming Principal of St Leonard's College in St Andrews in 1566.

Andrew Melville, in a following generation, enrolled in St Andrews at fourteen, and was soon hailed as the finest philosopher, poet or Grecian of any young master in the land. He taught oriental languages at Paris, became Principal of Glasgow University at the age of 25, and Principal of St Andrews in his thirties.

The Reformation did of course produce a massive advance. John Knox had the true passion for learning, and for everybody, of all classes. In his First Book of Discipline of 1560 he enjoined that schools should be erected in every parish for the instruction of youth in the principles of religion, grammar and Latin; that in small parishes a reader or minister should instruct the youth in the rudiments, especially

Above: Beginning work on new buildings for Edinburgh University in 1789.

Right: George Heriot, 1563-1624, hereditary goldsmith to the king in Edinburgh and royal money lender, left his fortune to found Heriot's Hospital which has now become Heriot's School.

the Catechism; that a college should be erected in every notable town in which logic and rhetoric should be taught along with learned languages. 'No father,' he said, 'is to be suffered to bring up his children according to his own fantasy, but all must be compelled to bring up their children in learning and virtue.'

And schooling remained firmly tied to the churches. State help and some funding did not arrive till nearly a century after the Reformation, in 1633. This did not inhibit Parliament from bringing in a compulsory education act in 1567, but it was a sadly impractical affair because the finance was not available to make it work. Not only that, at the Reformation the barons were very quick to take over the lands and property of the Roman Church, and the revenues that might have made widespread education practical went into private pockets.

The religious connection from then on was

not only still clear, but it was bedevilled by the up-and-down fortunes of religion itself. In 1606, Presbyterian government was abolished, and Episcopal government restored and formally established; as could be seen from the Education Act of 1616, which laid down that in every parish a school should be established and a fit person appointed to teach in the same upon the expense of the parish, at the site and by the advice of the bishop of the diocese.

Presbyterian government came back in 1638, and in spite of the to-ing and fro-ing of faiths, by the time of the Civil War, every village in Scotland had a school, almost every family had a Bible, and most children could read something of the Scripture..

This too had a fairly complex history. We may assume that the Scripture they read from their Bibles was in the noble and majestic English of the translation authorised by King James, Sixth of Scotland and First of England, who ascended the joint throne in 1603. But as far back as 1543 the Scottish Parliament, ignoring complaints from the Bishops, granted the people the privilege of reading the Bible in 'the vulgar toung, Inglis or Scottis.' There was a curious side-effect to the publication of the King James version, and one which was noticeable into modern times. It was, as we have seen elsewhere, the downgrading of the Scottish tongue.

It would also be wrong to see education as a homogeneous system. Despite the enactment of 1543, schoolboys in Aberdeen were strictly forbidden even to use their own native language, but were permitted only Latin, Greek, Hebrew, French or – and this is certainly curious – Gaelic.

The simple vision of total and universal education has to be amended by the fact of a lot of apathy among parents, whose children's time seemed more valuable at work to help

Right: Heriot's Hospital. Part of Heriot's fortune later helped found the Watt Institute, in 1852, which was to provide scientific teaching for ordinary working men. This organisation has now become Heriot Watt University.

support the family. And the swings and roundabouts were not over. Presbyterian government came back in 1638, but 22 years later came the Restoration of the merry monarch, Charles II, and the bishops were back in power, until the enthronement of William and Mary, when the Presbyterians were back again.

The Catholic Stewart dynasty was evidently gone forever. What the Presbyterian clergy wanted, in addition, was the total extirpation of Catholicism from the land. They had chosen the wrong man in King William. William of Orange was a live-and-let-live character. In his reign, it was ordained that teachers must subscribe to the Confession of Faith, and an inspectorate was established, not so much as to examine the efficiency of teachers, but to question professors, principals, regents and others to make sure that they did subscribe to the Confession, and the Oath of Allegiance, and to 'purge and remove' any who did not. It had the whiff of a witch-hunting organisation, but it soon fell into disuse in any case.

It was in this reign that the spread of schools really became complete, and from then on through the eighteenth century, Scotland did indeed lead the rest of Britain both in the quantity and quality of schooling. There were no doubt corners of apathy and truancy, but the institution was well established. Further education acts well into the century brought some kind of uniformity into the schools.

There were still aspects which seem bizarre and obscene when viewed from this distance. Teaching was a tolerably good job, with a guaranteed salary and often a house provided

as well, and the later laws found a simple rule-of-thumb method of coping with inflation, by tying the salaries to the going price of meal. But life for the pupils was by no means easy. It was laid down that a teacher might be dismissed on political grounds, or for inefficiency, or for excessive flogging. 'Excessive' meant flogging that resulted in the permanent deformity of a child, or its death.

Yet a report much later revealed a lot of ignorance and illiteracy among the natives of

Left: George (far left) and Thomas Hutcheson. Both left money for charitable works but the Hutchesons' school owes its origin to Thomas alone whose original benefaction provided for educating of 'twelve male children, indigent orphans or others of the like condition.'

Ross and Sutherland, and among Irish people who had settled there – though they all were enthusiastic that their children should be thoroughly educated. But as against that chilling reference to flogging, an inspector reported a fearful lack of discipline. He could not, he said, carry out an examination until half of the children had been put out of the school, since they were lolling about with hands in pockets and caps on heads, chattering endlessly and paying no attention whatever. Clearly, discipline, as well as the quality of education, varied from school to school.

The children who did pay attention, with or without corporal punishment, and their teachers, certainly had to work hard at it. The school day was ten hours, and it was not until the nineteenth century that it came down to six.

It is interesting that David Stow, the Paisley philanthropist who founded the Normal School in Glasgow in 1837 – the first teacher training college in the United Kingdom – was a passionate opponent of corporal punishment. His other enthusiasms were the abolition of prizes, and the mixing of sexes in schools.

By that time the Scottish universities were soundly established, well funded and with large rolls, and they were making their mark on the outside world, as Sir Walter Besant was later to proclaim. And they continued to throw up their intellectual giants. Joseph, later Lord, Lister, was English, a graduate at London University, but he did much of his greatest work at Edinburgh and Glasgow Universities, producing original research on the coagulation of blood and totally revolutionising the hit-and-miss art of surgery by his introduction of antiseptics.

James Clerk-Maxwell was an Edinburgh boy who took the high road to England, graduated from Cambridge and had chairs successively at Aberdeen, King's College London and Cambridge, where he organised the Cavendish Laboratory. At fifteen he produced a method of drawing oval curves which was published by the Royal Society of Edinburgh. As a man he published his seminal treatise on electricity and magnetism, produced original work on colour vision and the kinetic theory of gases, and electromagnetic radiation. He died at forty-eight.

William Thomson, Lord Kelvin, enrolled at Glasgow University when he was only eleven. After further study at Cambridge he returned to Glasgow as professor of natural philosophy and started to unravel the mysteries of electricity. His research made possible the laying of the Atlantic telegraph cable, but his life was a feverish outpouring of splendid things, electrical meters, sounding equipment; and of much insightful research into electrical theory.

Scotland was fertile ground for such masters. And although conditions for the working classes, especially in the cities, were fairly horrible, they saw education as an escape from the squalor and eagerly embraced it.

The situation remained fairly inchoate, all the same. From early in the nineteenth century there were parish schools, there were 'assembly schools' set up by the Church of Scotland, mainly in the scattered communities of the north, and the Church also established 'sessional schools' in the larger centres, in which the local kirk session was responsible for the building, the teacher, and the books. By 1860 Glasgow had over forty of these, and they were necessary. The population had risen from 77,000 in 1801 to nearly 400,000 in 1861.

Then there were the schools run by the 'breakaway' Free Church of Scotland after the split in 1843; episcopal schools; Roman Catholic schools; schools set up by the Scottish Society for the Propagation of Christian Knowledge; burgh schools and academies.

There were also, and this was a peculiarly Scottish phenomenon, the private adventure schools. Ordinary private schools, which pro-liferated in the nineteenth century, gave high-class education to the children of the wealthier classes. The adventure schools were little corners of enterprise, run by individuals with no particular qualifications – labourers, wea-vers, clerks and the like – as a means of liveli-hood. Glasgow in the 1880s had over eighty of them, catering for 7000 children. There were over 900 spread over the country.

The big landmark was the Education Act of 1872. It established compulsory education for children from five to thirteen, and the older schools were largely absorbed into the system.

It was not, in fact, free education. For many years after the Act, children paid a few coppers a week for the compulsory privilege, though this was merely a token contribution to the financing of the schools.

The private schools were financed by fees, though most were founded in the first place by inheritance or benefactions of wealthy indivi-duals, like Heriot's in Edinburgh, funded by the will of 'Jinglin' Geordie' Heriot – which specified education for 'poor fatherless boys, freemen's sons of the town of Edinburgh,' and the brothers George and Thomas Hutcheson of Glasgow, whose bounty was designed for the education of indigent male orphans. The evolution of such schools into establishments for the relatively rich is parallel to that of England's 'Public' Schools, meaning private schools. George Watson's in Edinburgh, Robert Gordon's in Aberdeen and many other notable institutions had similar beginnings and similar evolutions.

It is worth a glance at the financial situation of the teachers at the time of the Act. The average salary in a burgh school was £119 per annum, a very comfortable living for the period. The Rector of Edinburgh High School was paid £759, the English master of Glasgow High School £1,200.

Before leaving the subject of the inde-pendent schools, it is worth mentioning that between now and the present day, they have occasionally stimulated controversy by their simple existence. The view against them is that by their very existence they perpetuate social divisions, that they drain teaching resources from the state schools, that they do not repre-sent real freedom of choice since the freedom is confined to parents who can afford to pay fees.

The argument advanced in favour of the independent schools is that they are of good quality, that they set standards for the state schools to aspire to and that individuals have a democratic right to spend their money as they choose.

The schools have survived the controversy. And their abolition would hardly produce a transformation of the system. There are only 120 independent schools in the country, accounting for only two per cent of the pupil population. They seem to have a solid future. The adventure schools, on the other hand, faded away rapidly with the 1872 act.

But there were still problems, there would be further crises and controversies. One difficulty was that although Scotland now had a nation-ally organised system, the Scottish Education Department was actually a small committee in

Right: The Village School by Sir George Harvey, 1806-76.

Above: The Rev Thomas Guthrie teaching in his Ragged School in Princes Street, Edinburgh, 1857. The Ragged Schools were established to take education to the children of the very poor. Pupils sometimes undertook work like splitting kindling to help finance the schools. Guthrie's was the second school, after Sheriff Watson's pioneer establishment in Aberdeen in 1847.

If secondary education was having its troubles, there was still provision for ex-pupils who wanted to extend their horizons. 'Night school' became a powerful Scottish tradition, a programme of evening classes for young people above school age, who could find technical training geared to the local industries. The selection of courses also included language and literature.

For older people, there was an older tradition available, in the Mechanics Institution of Glasgow and the School of Arts in Edinburgh, which had been founded in the 1820s to give working men instruction in scientific principles. Both institutions flourished and consolidated, to be elevated to university status as Strathclyde in 1964 and Heriot-Watt in 1966.

The pioneering work of David Stow in Glasgow was recognised early in this century by the widespread introduction of teacher-training colleges. Previously, a university was regarded as sufficient experience for a teacher, but from 1906 professional training was introduced all round. Non-graduates were already obliged to take training courses.

There were now specialist subjects like art, music and domestic science which culminated in a teaching certificate. Later legislation required all male candidates for the Teacher's General Certificate to be university graduates, and this positively gave Scotland a unique position in the educational world, and one noticeably superior to England's, since every male teacher in the country had a university degree, and every teacher of higher classes in secondary schools was an honours graduate. Local committees for the training of teachers took over the old church training centres and laid the ground for the establishment of the modern training colleges of Moray House in Edinburgh, the Aberdeen and Dundee colleges, and Jordanhill in Glasgow.

Education, like every other social service, was badly damaged by the Great War. Huge numbers of young male teachers were called to the Forces, and the schools were demoralised. Many of the older boys felt that they too should be fighting men. Many lied about their ages and did go to that devastating war. Others saw the chance of making good wages in war factories. Truancy was common. For those who stuck to their desks, the war was also a hard time, with fuel shortages and weary teachers dragged back from retirement.

But the war was going to culminate, in Lloyd George's empty phrase, in a land fit for heroes to live in. Indeed, the idealistic urge to reward the survivors for their sacrifice did result in a plan for higher education for ex-service personnel, and 6,000 students benefited from it in its first five years. It also helped to inspire the visionary Scottish Education Act of 1918. Education was to be improved, extended, and brought up to date with the changed times.

London. It was not until 1885 that public pressure resulted in the creation of the government minister the Secretary for Scotland, and not until 1939 that his offices were moved to Edinburgh.

The new system still had its deficiencies. Children proving their proficiency in reading, writing and arithmetic were entitled to leave school before the age of thirteen, a process that went on until 1901. In 1883 the leaving age was raised to fourteen, but pupils could opt for half-time education from the age of ten.

The concentration on elementary education actually also had a damaging effect on secondary education. The school boards who administered the education rates had no powers to spend any of them on secondary teaching. When money was made available, it was channelled through too many separate organisations, and the result was a confusion which would last for decades.

Also, education did not exist in a vacuum. The children were members of a society which was not perfect and not equal, but stained with poverty, undernourishment and the ills that went with it. Schools became involved in the physical health of their children, and an act of 1908 introduced regular medical inspection and permitted school boards to give meals to children who were in need of them.

Unfortunately, the times quite quickly changed for the worse with the postwar slump. Far from extending the system, the Scottish Education Department was forced to call for economies. The scheme for compulsory further education was quietly forgotten.

One provision did come into effect, by which Roman Catholic schools would henceforth be maintained from the rates, but retain their independence, a notable demonstration of generous tolerance when we recall the outright persecution of Catholic education for centuries after the Reformation. In the eighteenth century the SSPCK had insistently called on the law to suppress Catholic schools entirely. In Banffshire, a crude turf shed housing a seminary for priests was reduced to the ground three times by the military, and when a new substantial stone building was put in its place, it was burned down.

This clause in the 1918 Act, then, did seem to herald an age of tolerance, of live-and-let-live. And it is so, for most of the Scottish people. But there were many non-Catholics, and there are still some, who resented what they saw as privilege given to the Catholic community. There are others who take the view that the separation of the communities in youth merely deepens the divisions.

The common terms are Catholic schools and Protestant schools, but the non-Catholic schools are properly called non-denominational schools, and indeed many city schools today have large Muslim populations.

Above: As the city of Glasgow developed the university was moved from its original site in High Street to its present position in Gilmorehill. The photograph shows the main university building.

Since religion (once again) impinges on education, it should be said that Scotland, and particularly the central belt, has indeed demonstrated fierce antagonism between the two communities, at their outer fringes, and it has erupted into violence in the context of that other great institution, Association Football, with pitched battles between supporters of Glasgow Rangers and Glasgow Celtic. There has been a distinct lessening of that trouble in recent years, and a recent Papal visit to Glasgow provoked no disagreeable incidents.

Until recent years, some ambitious Roman Catholic parents chose to send their children to non-denominational secondary schools because, although prospective employers would hesitate to show prejudice by inquiring about an applicant's religion, the name of the school would immediately reveal it. This practice is also fading away.

There are, however, still cases of adjacent Catholic and non-denominational schools whose headmasters arrange jointly to stagger break times to avoid clashes among the pupils. In Scotland, religious enthusiasm can still spill over into sectarian excess. In the 1950s, a black American musician visiting the country expressed his admiration of the total absence of a colour bar. It was explained to him that Glaswegians did not need to discriminate against blacks when there were so many Catholics available.

Left: A poster by the watercolour artist Agnes Raeburn advertising the Glasgow Lecture Association, dating from 1897. The Lecture Association was active from 1895-1906 and brought eminent lecturers to speak in Glasgow.

After the slump of 1919, Scotland's economic situation improved slightly through the 1920s, but the educational system did no more than hold the line. This in itself was a matter of some pride. It was common for pupils whose families moved to England to discover that they were fully a year ahead of their contemporaries in the south. The Wall Street Crash of 1929, however, brought other economies with it, and by the thirties, schoolteachers were being obliged to accept reduced salaries as an alternative to unemployment. Those emerging from training colleges could no longer expect to be offered a job at once. In this, they shared the experience of most Scots, including the young people who had left school to join the queue of the unemployed.

One result was the emergence of the short-lived Junior Instruction Centres, classes for the young unemployed designed to give training in various subjects, to keep them interested, and in short, to keep them off the streets. They existed in Glasgow, Aberdeen, Greenock and Motherwell, and did their best. To the pupils, they were the Buroo Schools, named from the Employment Bureaux, which were known to their clients as the Unemployment Bureaux.

The outbreak of the Second World War was much more shattering than that of the First. The bomber, as Mr Stanley Baldwin had warned, would always get through, and children and teachers from the target cities were evacuated. It was a massive operation, thousands of children with gas-mask cases strung from their necks, identity cards pinned to their coats, boarding trains and buses to remote little towns and villages to be chosen by householders as permanent boarders. For some, it was a wonderful new experience of rural and village life. For some it was only heartbreak.

The enormous evacuation programme was organised by the wartime government with the best of intentions and in the certain knowledge that Scotland's cities would be unsafe for children. In the event, the bomber got through to Clydebank for only two days, in a sortie that left a handful of bombs on Glasgow. As the war went on, many children drifted back to their city homes, but as in World War I, education had been one of the first casualties.

Something not generally known was that throughout the 1930s, secondary education was, in law, not free. The pupils were liable to pay a small sum for this privilege. In practice, it was free. The pupils of the thirties were never asked for the coppers paid by their ancestors under the Education Act of 1872, and even before World War II broke out, most of them had their books free.

Again, after the war, the educational people were ready to transform the school scene. They had a problem. From being a leader in the world of education, Scotland had developed rigid ideas on the subject. It was absolutely

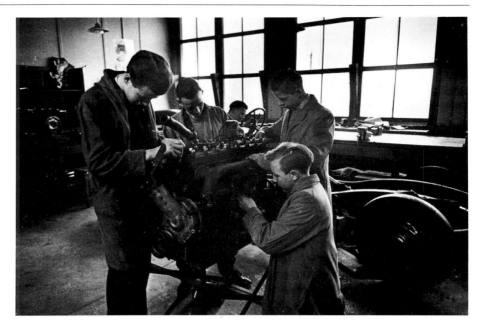

Above: Scene in a Junior Instruction Centre or 'Buroo School' in 1939.

committed to the three Rs, Reading, Riting, Rithmetic. With all its magical passion for innovation, Scotland is also the country in which a learned professor in the late nineteenth century could write:

'The truth is that the intellect of women is a very difficult growth, and that it is interwoven with her imagination, her affection, and her moral emotions much more intimately than in man. What the world wants is not two men, a big one in trousers and a little one in petticoats, but a man and a woman.'

Ten years after World War II, an educationalist could write, 'It would appear that Scotland, which had a national system of education when England was merely groping in the dark, has been marking time or even falling behind.'

Nevertheless, the wartime experience brought benefits in the attitude to welfare services. It is an ironic fact that the mass of British people, including most children, enjoyed a better balanced diet under wartime rationing than they had in all the years before. The war had also increased the provision of welfare arrangements in Scottish schools, with an expanded meals service and as in the 1914-18 conflict, people looked to a brave new world when the war was over, and planned for it. The result was the Education Act of 1945.

All education in public schools was to be free by law as well as in practice, and that included free books and writing materials.

The new forward-looking attitude produced two trends, which were clearly in the name of progress but which were not universally applauded. One was an increase in the school years. The leaving age was raised from the prewar 14 to 15 in 1947, and to 16 in 1972. The theory is simple; children who spend longer at school will acquire more education. In general, the theory has been vindicated. But children vary as much as adults, and for many pupils, ROSLA, the raising of the school leaving age, just meant an extended sentence in a place they regarded as a prison. This had an effect on education itself. The schools had to become more flexible, to provide classes that would keep non-academic older pupils from becoming bored and rebellious.

The other trend was to egalitarianism. In prewar days, the Qualifying Examination at the end of the primary course divided the academically quick from the others, the first group going to a Higher Grade secondary and the rest to shorter courses in Advanced Division schools, with classes in woodwork and other practical subjects, in preparation for the artisan life.

It was a crude mechanism, it was socially divisive in a minor way, splitting up groups of primary school friends. Many academically gifted pupils taking French and Latin and higher mathematics, incidentally resented not being introduced to the cheerier charms of woodwork.

Under the new Acts, children of both categories went automatically to the same schools. The wide variation in ability was handled by the process of streaming, which was basically the old system under one roof and a new name. But what was now called comprehensive education was a reality.

It was also a political battleground. Many parents in the postwar period, in choosing where to live, were less interested in the new house itself than in how near it was to a school they regarded as of good quality. In the fifties and sixties there were long waiting lists for Scotland's fee-paying schools, filled with what are now known as the upwardly mobile, who were now following another old Scottish tradition of the wealthy and the nobility, who ever since the Union of the Crowns have sent their sons to boarding schools, usually in England.

At the same time there arose a vigorous campaign for the abolition of the tawse, the heavy leather strap then still used for corporal punishment in Scottish schools. Though the campaign involved some teachers, a great many others viewed it with distrust. The use of the tawse had already decreased in any case, and the ferocious beatings of olden times, the sometimes excessive application between the wars, were simply no longer acceptable to society.

One educationalist, opposed to abolition, put his views very moderately. 'Thousands of teachers,' he said, 'teach from one year to the next either without recourse, or with minimum recourse, to corporal punishment, and then usually in cases of extreme provocation, flagrant breach of rules, or where to fail to take this step would endanger other pupils or undermine the work of the school. The great majority of Scottish teachers operate under a system of discipline which is firm, fair and benevolent; the great majority of Scottish classrooms are pleasant places in which children live and work.'

In vain. The mood of the times was against the tawse, though the world was living in violent times. That statement was made in 1972. Very soon, the tawse was officially abandoned in Scottish schools.

It is not too easy to analyse the effects. The ultimate sanction of physical punishment had diminished, but to many teachers, the disappearance of the ultimate sanction meant the loss of discipline. Teachers' jobs in the eighties are much less attractive than they were in the heady decades after the war. Teaching is no longer the secure, attractive job it was after the Act of 1872.

The difficulties should not be exaggerated, but it is very difficult for many teachers to maintain discipline in the classroom without that disagreeable final resort, a resort which most pupils accepted fairly philosophically.

Also, the situation on the financial ladder of society steadily worsened during the late 1970s and 1980s. In the thirties, school-teachers were among the few people who could own cars. In the 1980s, teachers in Scotland recall the situation of teachers before the Act of 1872, many of whom needed part-time enterprises, like organising cockfights, in order to make a living.

In our time, the once important Scottish school-teacher has been one of the favoured members of society. The proud old tradition is under threat, and we have seen the unpredictable phenomenon of teachers' strikes.

But this is what history is about. There never comes a time when a fine tradition becomes a permanency. Scottish education (second to none, as one old enthusiast said) is in a state of flux. It will always be. History is the story of change.

Below: Striking teachers demonstrate in 1986. The long lasting teachers' dispute certainly hit the education of many young Scots but it may have helped in the longer term by directing public attention to solving the many problems which schools face.

9 Improvements and Clearances

THROUGHOUT THE centuries, Scotland acquired a rich mixture of races through invasion and immigration, and the newcomers were absorbed into a fairly homogeneous breed. The forms of speech varied widely between, say, Aberdeenshire in the north-east and Ayrshire in the south-west, but the differences were largely of accent. They were all forms of English, or the subdivision known as Scots-English, and that is the situation today.

One curious fact is that while the Scots, or at least the working-class Scots, use this form as the spoken tongue, they write in English. It is worth pausing to examine this dichotomy. The Authorised translation of the Bible was made in the south of England, in the language of that area and in the majestic seventeenth century style, as we already know; and this helped to introduce, or impose, 'Standard' English as the written language. There have been periods between then and now when many Scots have tried to eradicate the Scottishness of their speech, feeling that it was somehow lower-class than Standard, even while they revered the Scots poetry of Robert Burns, usually briefly, once a year, around the date of his birthday on 25 January.

In our time the old Scots tongue, though much of the vocabulary has vanished from common speech, is enjoying a revival and a new respectability, and there is a large school of new poets using it and enjoying wide acceptance. The history of language is a very emotional and complex one, changing constantly and even faster than the history of those who use it.

One group of Scots, however, stubbornly remained outside of this homogenizing process; the Gaels. Their ancient language, and its cousins in Ireland, Wales, Brittany in France and to a small extent in Cornwall, are descended, like most languages on the Continent, from the lost tongue of Indo-European. For some reason it tended to move, or to be driven, to the western extremities of Europe, and, like its people, it has regularly been under threat. Estimates today are that it is spoken by a mere 100,000 Scots, out of a population of over four million. There are signs that it is consolidating and even expanding since some children in Lowland schools study it as a second language.

But the divide has always been there, and remains. Gaelic children in the Highlands and Islands also learn English – Standard English rather than Scots-English. Nevertheless, the country is separated by language and culture, into the English-speaking Lowlands and the Gaelic-speaking Highlands and Islands.

The division was even deeper in older times, and played a part in the bleak tragedy of the Highland Clearances, which were to denude the land of many of its people and leave great areas bare and deserted.

The process begins with the failed rebellion in 1745 of Bonnie Prince Charlie, and the slaughter of his Highland troops at Culloden, near Inverness. In the aftermath, the Duke of Cumberland, the victorious English commander, launched a campaign to root out any lingering traces of rebellion. Great numbers of people in the Highlands, men, women and children, were killed on suspicion of disloyalty to the Government, or even on the general principle that the only good Highlander was a dead Highlander. Their outlandish language and their alien customs made it possible to regard them as Other, as less than full human beings.

It is a psychological twist that has justified the urge to colonise. The American Indians also suffered from it. In the case of the Highlands it has an even blacker tinge since the victims, in spite of their language, were compatriots of the killers, and that the killers had no intention of taking over the rather forbidding land and settling it; they were merely engaged in an act of violence for its own sake.

And when that was over, there were more dark days to come. The Government in London wanted to extinguish everything that made the

Previous page: Detail from *The Last of the Clan* by Thomas Faed, 1826-1900. Although Faed lived in London for a large part of his life (he was born in Kircudbright) many of his paintings deal in a romantic style with Scottish themes such as this scene of emigration.

Below: The 6th Earl of Haddington, painted here by Sir John Baptiste de Medina, was in political life a supporter of the Union with England, but also known as a keen agricultural improver.

Gaels different and distinctive. In the Black Act of 1746, as it was known to the Highlanders and Islanders, they were forbidden to own arms, which was reasonable enough, but also to wear the kilt or any garments of tartan cloth, and offenders could be transported to Botany Bay. Some were.

But apart from the London Government, the natives soon found other forces of oppression among them, in the shape of their own chieftains, or sometimes other landlords to whom the chieftains sold out. There were edicts in some areas actually forbidding marriages among estate tenants. In the parish of Clyne in Sutherlandshire a few years later, there were 75 bachelors aged from 35 to 75.

Then, in 1846 and 1847, came the failure of the potato crop through the same blight that devastated Ireland in the Hungry Forties and reduced its population to a fraction. Though not the sole staple of the Highlanders the potato provided most of their nourishment, and the natives starved. The situation was so desperate that it did cause concern outside of the Highlands, and public meetings were held to discuss ways of helping, though one Highland landlord said at the time that there was nothing seriously wrong and that the peasants were no worse off than they had been for a quarter of a century.

Something like £300,000 was raised for relief; but there was to be no reckless generosity towards the hungry. Lord Trevelyan, appointed commissioner to administer the fund, decreed that the able-bodied were not to be given food without working for it, at the rate of a pound of meal for ten hours' labour.

There were other odd twists in the administration, like the case of Lord MacDonald, who generously contributed £1,000 to the fund and received £3,000 as his share to be distributed as he thought fit. The Sutherland family contributed £6,000 and received £21,000, A large share of this was spent on building a hunting lodge, miles from any starving peasants. Quantities of food were stored, for sale to the victims, and some of it went bad and was used for fodder.

It should be realised that before Culloden, a Highland chief drew his pride and importance from the number of loyal clansmen who would follow him into battle, and history had provided plenty of battles. And the clansmen, from all the evidence, were equally proud to be called and to die gloriously if necessary.

In the new situation there was no basis for that pride. The chief, who in some cases had been merely the spokesman and military commander, sometimes actually elected rather than hereditary, now found himself strictly a landlord, with the necessity, like all landlords, of getting as much rent as he could. And within a few decades of Culloden, a majority of the chiefs could no longer be bothered living in the

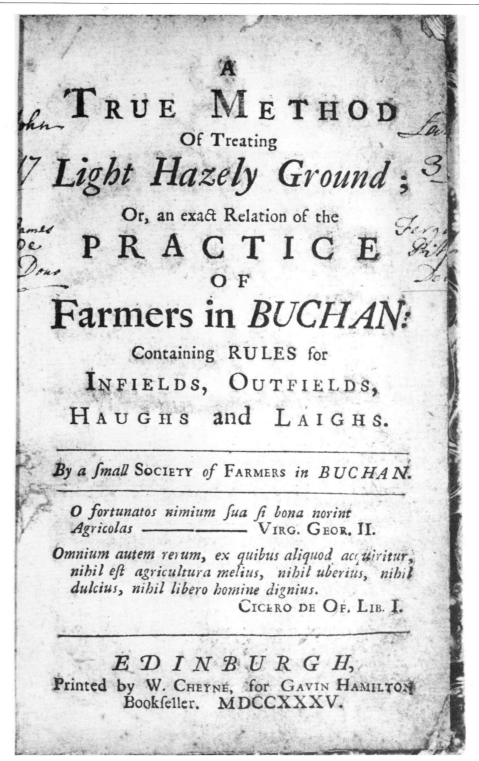

clan land, but preferred city society; an expensive hobby for men drawing petty rents. The solution was to be the process they called The Improvements.

The Highlander, although he had always paid tribute to the chief in cash or kind, regarded the land as his own. It was not. Chieftains had underlings, tacksmen, or factors, who held leases on areas of land, paid rent to the laird and took rent from the peasants. When the tacksmen's rents were raised, the increase was passed down the line, and if there were any problems, the tacksmen's leases could be ended. And the tacksmen too had

Above: The desire to increase agricultural yields led to the establishment of many scientific societies in the eighteenth century. The hope of emulating the success which such groups helped bring to Lowland farms was to play a part in the changes which led to the Clearances in the Highlands.

their social positions to maintain. But the laird lost nothing in losing a tacksman. There were others who could pay better rents; Lowland sheep farmers. Steadily the glens began to be emptied of people and populated with Cheviot sheep.

The peasants were not actually driven from Scotland. They were moved to miserable little plots on the rocky coastlines to scrape a living from miserable smallholdings and fishing; and, quite often, die.

This contempt for the faithful clansmen was not entirely novel. Even before Culloden, one or two lairds who were anxious to get into lucrative trade had dabbled in slaving. Sir Alexander MacDonald of Sleat and Norman MacLeod of Dunvegan actually got into the trade by selling some of their clansmen into bondage in the Carolinas.

Some contemporaries blamed the ordinary Highlander for his own plight, and there is some justice in this view. The old loyalty was deeply ingrained, and although he might willingly attack outsiders at the chief's order, he could not attack or rebel against the chief himself. He submitted to the callousness of the laird.

And it was a heavy burden. To move to the coast he had to take his dwelling with him, or at least the roof timbers, since there were virtually no trees in the area. But for some, there was another removal available – removal to the New World. In one year, 1772, over six thousand people left Inverness-shire and Ross to sail to the Americas. It was only the beginning.

It was a year later that Doctor Samuel Johnson made his celebrated pilgrimage to Scotland, and found that, 'The clans retain little of

And they were. In 1801, 830 people emigrated. In 1802, eleven ships carrying 3,300 passengers sailed from the Hebrides alone. By 1803, twenty thousand people were preparing to flee to America. In one estate in Skye, they included 150 families out of 153 families; on another, the entire population of 2,000.

Suddenly the situation began to worry the Government, and the great Scottish engineer, Thomas Telford, creator of the Caledonian Canal, was sent north to study the causes of emigration and recommend ways of discouraging it. He reported quite simply that the most significant cause was the conversion of large tracts of land into sheep farms.

The official response certainly helped, though it did nothing very significant for the peasantry. It was the passing of the Passenger Vessels Act of 1803, which put a legal limit on the number of passengers to be carried in ships of various sizes. The effect was to raise the price of a passage from £4 to £10, too high for most of the despairing Highlanders

They had a brief relief when recruiting agents for the Canadian Fencibles Regiment visited the Highlands in 1804 with the alluring offer of a position in the regiment, free passage for the recruit and his family, and the free gift of a plot of land after discharge from the army.

Emigration was a large part of the reason for commissioning Telford to organise the creation of the great Canal, and of roads here and there in the Highlands, but they only nibbled at the problem, and the norm remained the wretched seaside crofts, whose inhabitants actually had to create little patches of farmland, the machairs, with sand and seaweed.

The name Patrick Sellar is perhaps the most infamous in this long woeful tale. He was factor to the Sutherland family, and a man of boundless enthusiasm. The Countess of Sutherland had married the Earl of Stafford, and used both titles. Sellar wrote:

'Lord and Lady Stafford were pleased humanely to order the new arrangement of this country. That the interior should be possessed by Cheviot shepherds, and the people brought down to the coast and places in lots of less than three acres, sufficient for the maintenance of an industrious family, pinched enough to cause them to turn their attention to the fishing. A most benevolent action, to put these barbarous Highlanders into a position where they could better associate together, apply themselves to industry, educate their children, and advance in civilisation.'

The fish referred to were herring. The scene was the same in Wester Ross and elsewhere. The crofters were cheap labour, and surprisingly, crofting went together with a population growth.

The cheap labour force was for the gathering of kelp, which could well have been used by the crofters as fertiliser for their little plots. It was

Above: Highland Chieftain by John Michael Wright. This picture, painted in about 1680, is one of the earliest of a man in Highland costume.

their original character. Their military ardour is extinguished, their dignity of independence is depressed, their contempt for Government is subdued, and their reverence for their chiefs abated.'

Their lack of reverence was matched by the chiefs'. The old clan lands were to be worked by the highest bidder. And even on the rocky shorelines, the peasant was not to be his own man. There was the matter of kelp, the flourishing seaweed among the rocks, and at times it was an even more profitable product than sheep. The lairds, naturally, assumed ownership of it. During the brief season in April and May the peasants gathered it, for poverty wages.

One irony was that kelp-gathering needed a huge labour force while the people were constantly being reduced in number. As one laird commented, 'If the country has any inhabitants at all, they must be expelled.'

not. It was the landlord's property, and theft of it from the shore was punished by eviction. What the lairds wanted it for was for sale to industry, which used it as a source of alkali in the making of glass and soap.

In what could seem like an act of benevolent paternalism, the chieftain MacNeill of Barra actually built an alkali works on the island, with the kilns to reduce the raw material and provide some local industrial employment. To raise the capital for this humanitarian project, he divided every croft on the island into two equal halves, and charged the same rent for the halves as he had collected for the original croft. It could be that he was a true Highlander himself, in the sense that Lowlanders believe Highlanders are strangers to the hard discipline of entrepreneurial activities. The kelp trade had started to decline several years before his ambitious scheme, and very soon he was bankrupt. For 500 of his tenants, it did not matter, since they had emigrated as soon as he introduced the half-croft scheme. It was unfortunate for 500 other tenants who had come from other islands to take their places. The estate was taken over at MacNeill's collapse by

Gordon of Cluny, who soon had a less imaginative but more efficient idea of transporting his excess peasants, whether they liked it or not, to Canada.

There are less gloomy sidelights on the Highland history, and one of them concerns the ancient Highland garb which was proscribed in 1746.

The law had been repealed in 1782, partly because the rest of Britain was discovering that the Highlanders were a romantic breed. This development was confirmed by Walter Scott's best-selling novels which glorified such characters as the rebel Rob Roy MacGregor. Well-bred Lowlanders acquired the habit of tracing Highland ancestry, however remote, and wearing kilts to show their family connections.

When King George IV made his state visit to Edinburgh in 1812, the kilt was high fashion for important occasions. The King himself, though his Gaelic connections were obscure at best, had a kilt made, and with his enormous obesity made a colourful spectacle.

The kilt to be worn by a man, then as now, had properly to be made from the particular

Below left: An illustration from a pamphlet published in 1742 showing a soldier of the Black Watch, the first Highland regiment.

Below: A commission to the Earl of Seaforth authorising the raising of a regiment for service during the American War of Independence in 1778.

GEORGE R.

WHEREAS, We have thought fit to order a HIGHLAND REGIMENT OF FOOT to be forthwith raifed under your Command; to confift of Ten Companies, of Five Serjeants, Five Corporals, Two Drummers, and One Hundred Private Men in each Company; with Two Pipers to the Grenadier-Company, befides Commiffioned Officers.——Thefe are to authorife You, by Beat of Drum or otherwife, to raife fo many Men, in any County or Part of Our Kingdom of GREAT BRITAIN, as fhall be wanting to complete the faid Regiment to the above-mentioned Numbers.——And all Magiftrates, Juftices of the Peace, Conftables, and other Our Civil Officers whom it may concern, are hereby required to be affifting unto you in providing Quarters, impreffing Carriages, and otherwife as there fhall be Occafion. Given at Our Court at St JAMES's, this Eighth Day of JANUARY 1778, in the Eighteenth Year of Our Reign.

By His MAJESTY's COMMAND,

BARRINGTON.

To

Our Right Trufty and Right Well-Beloved Coufin, KENNETH, Earl of SEAFORTH, Lieutenant-Colonel Commandant of a *Highland Regiment of Foot* to be forthwith raifed, or to the Officer appointed to raife Men for Our faid *Regiment*.

A True Copy.

M. LEWIS.

tartan of his remote clan ancestors. It was not always so, even during the King's visit. But soon afterwards, there arrived in Edinburgh two brothers, John and Charles Sobieski Stuart, who made it known that they were grandsons of Bonnie Prince Charlie. They were educated, and charming, and soon became the darlings of upper-class society in the Capital.

In one of the numerous Edinburgh houses which gave them hospitality, his hostess noticed that John was fascinated by a tartan bedspread, and privately told a friend that he would soon be wearing it. She was right, but more, John revealed that he had a Latin manuscript detailing the exact and correct patterns for the tartans of all the old clans.

Walter Scott himself was very doubtful, and wanted a look at the manuscript. The brothers refused to let it out of their possession, but when he was allowed a brief glance at one page, he found the Latin full of small errors. John Sobieski Stuart later claimed that he had been able to compare his copy with another in the Augustine Monastery in Cadiz, and to prove its authenticity. The brothers published a text as *Vestiarium Scoticum*, and it was an instant success. To this day, Scotsmen, Englishmen, Americans and others with Scottish forebears, are careful to buy tartans of their own family pattern and will wear no other. It is a harmless and colourful industry.

The old clansmen did not even wear a kilt shaped as we know it, pleated at the back, strapped round the waist and reaching the knees – the philibeg, or short kilt. Their common garb was the long kilt, which was simply a piece of woollen cloth, two yards by six yards, made of plaid material using any natural dyes available to their womenfolk. It was used as a bedroll at night when the owner was away from home. In daytime, it was laid on the ground over a waist-belt and then pleated. The owner next lay on it, pulled one end over his shoulder and down the front of his body, and finally fastened the belt around it.

One observer, Sir John Sinclair, declared that the new form of kilt which we know today, with permanent pleats, was invented by an Englishman in 1770. Such facts, if it is a fact, cannot stand in the way of popular tradition, however new.

The romantic revival did nothing for the Highlanders themselves. Patrick Sellar, whose name is still remembered with loathing in the Highlands, was enthusiastically evicting Sutherland tenants in Farr and Kildonan. He had ordered them in 1814 to give up their holdings by the May term, and to make life even more uncomfortable, he and his men harried them by setting fire to the heath grazing before the date, to starve the cattle.

Left: Highland Music by Sir Edwin Landseer, who painted many romanticised Highland scenes.

Above: In former times, as today, lack of opportunity caused many young people to move away from the Highland areas. Finding work in domestic service was one common avenue in the past. This photograph shows the servants of a Perthshire country house around 1890.

Napoleon was spending his Hundred Days on Elba at the time, Europe was at peace, and suddenly there was little demand for exports of cattle, and the luckless tenants had to sell their beasts for practically nothing, while Sellar's new tenants' cattle invaded the arable land. In this eviction, most of the victims had no chance even to strip the roof timbers of their homes to take with them, because Sellar put the houses (which the tenants had built for themselves) to the torch.

There were deaths and injuries. One Mrs John M'Kay, trying to dismantle her home before the arsonists could get to it, fell through the roof and had premature labour. Donald McBeath had his roof ripped off and died of exposure. One old woman's bedclothes were set alight, she was rescued with difficulty and carried to a barn, where she died five days later. 'Damn her, the old witch, she's lived too long,' said Sellar, according to a witness.

One tenant, Hugh McBeth, sought an interview in advance with Sellar, and told him that he had to leave for his godmother's funeral, asked that his house and his sick elderly father might be left alone until he came back. Sellar sent him packing. McBeth partially demolished the cottage before leaving, hoping that this would satisfy the factor. When he came back he found the house destroyed and his sick father lying in the open, to die very soon.

At one burning, a cat ran out from the flames, was grabbed and thrown back. Crowds of people slept on the bare hillsides, watching the embers of their homes.

One of the witnesses of these exciting times was Donald MacLeod, who was so incensed that he spent much of his life writing tracts and essays and furious letters to Edinburgh newspapers, to give the truth of the events. He put much of his writings together in his book *Gloomy Memories*, which is still a major source for historians investigating the times. The title is interesting. Harriet Beecher Stowe, of *Uncle Tom's Cabin* fame, visited Britain and was elegantly entertained by the Sutherlands. The author who had cried out against the injustice of American slavery was quite enchanted by her aristocratic British friends, and totally convinced of their warm humanity towards the little people of Sutherlandshire, and wrote a little book on the Highlands called *Happy Memories*. The title incensed MacLeod, and he never stopped correcting the record, or trying to, even after he eventually emigrated to Canada.

And astonishingly, Patrick Sellar was brought to court to be tried. Astonishingly, because the political climate of the time was one of terror at any activity of the lower classes on the political scene. The French Revolution had raised spectres of bloody rebellion and dispossession.

Liberty was a dangerous word. It was not a word much used in the Highlands, where the people were so remote that they were shielded from dangerous European heresies. It had infected England and the Lowlands of Scotland, particularly Scotland, where a body of freedom-lovers had previously formed a Society of the Friends of the People, whose leader, Thomas Muir of Huntershill, was sentenced to transportation.

And so it is astonishing that Sellar was charged at all. He was, after all, the agent of the respectable people of Britain, the landlords. Even so, the trial was delayed for nearly a year. The witnesses against him, forty of them, had been interviewed by Sheriff-Substitute M'Kid, but only fifteen were called to give evidence. There were nine witnesses on Sellar's behalf, all of them his own men. The case was heard in Inverness before Lord Pitmilly.

The Judge, in his summing-up to the jury, leant heavily on the low character of the chief prosecution witness, a tinker, William Chisholm who had seen his mother-in-law die during the evictions. The jury, solidly middle-class, took only a quarter of an hour to bring in a verdict of Not Guilty. Sheriff-Substitute M'Kid was driven from office, and even sued by Sellar, and simply disappeared.

But it was the famine of the 1840s that started the emptying of the Highlands. The landlords,

including the second Duke of Sutherland, were stung to compassion. He gave nearly £80,000 to relieve starvation. Nothing was enough. And while food was being distributed in meagre amounts, food was actually being exported from the Eastern Highlands. The locals on some occasions physically prevented ships at ports like Macduff and Banff from being loaded with grain for the south.

There were fewer and fewer of them to protest. Even before the famine, in 1831, 58,000 people emigrated to Canada. A year later, more than 60,000.

The law limiting the number of passengers per ship had been abandoned in 1827, and the conditions of the emigrants were appalling. In one year, a third of the British emigrants, penned below decks with no sanitation, contracted typhus, and a great many died before they could see the New World.

The Government, which had once tried to find ways of preventing the depopulation of the Highlands, now wanted the area emptied, and all its troubles off its hands. It stopped short of providing the money for the scheme. One official, visiting the departure of a ship from Glasgow, was disturbed that the Highland emigrants all looked strong and healthy. He had assumed that the purpose of the emigrations was to rid the Highlands of the poor, the sick and the useless.

At the same time, the forcible evictions were going on, and even the London *Times* suddenly became aware of them. The great editor of the 'Thunderer', Delane, was startled by an advertisement submitted to the paper by a Scottish solicitor, declaring that ninety peasants in Ross-shire had been driven from their homes

Below: Harvest time on a Perthshire farm in the 1880s. Both photographs on this page are the work of Magnus Jackson who was a well-known landscape photographer of the time as well as a town councillor in Perth.

Left: A magazine illustration from 1853 showing the loading of a ship with emigrants from the Isle of Skye.

and might have to take refuge in the local churchyard, without shelter. A *Times* reporter was sent north to report on the miseries of the cottagers of Glencalvie.

They were indeed in the churchyard, and they included twenty-three children, several of them sick. All of them simply disappeared from history.

And soon history, and London newspapers, were more concerned with the war against Russia than with the mundane problems of the Highlanders. And so there were no reports of

Below: Flood in the Highlands by Sir Edwin Landseer. From the 1820s Landseer painted many sumptuous scenes from Highland life, particularly wildlife. This helped inspire Victorian interest in the Highlands as a hunting ground. Unfortunately estates given over to raising deer had even less need of local workers than hills farmed for sheep.

the bloody affair in Strathcarron, in Ross-shire, where the landlord James Gillanders had planned to clear the glen in private.

The tenants had their suspicions, and the women were militant, as they had been in other places earlier in the long struggle. Summonses of evictions were delivered in 1854 by a band led by Alexander Munro, who had already assured the people that no eviction was planned. But on a signal from their lookouts, the women of the glen left their homes to intercept a Sheriff's Officer and his deputy.

The two claimed later that they had been attacked, stripped and beaten by a disorderly mob. A few days later two other officers, rather drunk, marched into the glen to deliver the eviction notices. One of them drew a pistol and aimed it at one of the women, whose young son produced an old useless gun and threatened him with death.

The intruders fled, with a hysterical report of savage crowds engaged in deforcement, a Scottish phrase meaning the removal of legal power from law officers. The next invasion of the glen was altogether more powerful and numerous. It was met by a crowd of sixty women. When the women refused to stand aside, the Sheriff in charge lost his temper and ordered his men to knock the women down.

The police charged into the crowd, swinging their truncheons at the women's heads and kicking those who fell. One middle-aged woman who tried to remonstrate with the police force and show the Sheriff a letter promising that no evictions were to be made, was clubbed down by three officers, who jumped on her inert body and stamped on her face.

The husbands were strangely absent during all of this. The officers were carried away in a hysterical attack on any woman near to hand. One of the few male peasants present, a man of sixty-eight who was merely watching, was beaten to the ground with truncheons and savagely kicked as he lay.

Four of the injured women were taken back to Tain, in chains, to be charged as ring-leaders of the mob. In the end, two people were charged, Ann Ross and Peter Ross, whose part in the incident was obscure. She was jailed for a year, and he sent to hard labour for eighteen months. The judge, Lord Justice Clerk Hope, mentioned 'a perverted feeling in some districts of the Highlands against the removal of tenants. This is most prejudicial to the interests of all and must be suppressed.'

The outbreaks of brutality, the tales of individual greed, are only dramatic embellishments of a dreary process of something akin to genocide. Undramatically, the process went on and on.

In 1886, after determined action by the Highlanders, particularly on the Island of Skye, there was a very tardy Government response in

Below: A Scotch Fair by John Philip, 1817-67. Note the recruiting tent for a Highland regiment in the background.

the shape of the Crofting Act, which gave the smallholders of the Highlands and Islands perpetual security of their little plots. But the reduction of their numbers went on in other ways. In World War I, and indeed in World War II, it was common for all the young men of a Highland township to enlist in the same regiment; and in the holocaust of the Great War, the entire fit male population of marriageable age in a township could be destroyed in a single action in France. The Highlanders were much admired by Army commanders for their strength, courage and unquestioning discipline. And they died.

They were not alone, of course. In Glasgow in that war, there were parades and jubilation when virtually the entire young manpower of the Glasgow tramway system answered, en bloc, the stirring cry of Lord Kitchener, Secretary for War, 'Your Country Needs You!' Few of them returned.

For many other Highlanders, Glasgow by that time was home. It was easier to migrate there than abroad. Today there are more of their kinsmen's descendants in the city than there are in the Highlands. More in Nova Scotia, where the old language still flourishes. More elsewhere in Canada, in America and the Antipodes. They have thriven, they have assimilated. But even more than the emigrants from Lowland Scotland, they have an umbilical attachment to the land their ancestors left.

From the lone shieling of the misty island
Mountains divide us, and the waste of seas
But still the blood is strong, the heart is
   Highland
And we in dreams behold the Hebrides.

Throughout the last century, the pressure to emigrate from the Highlands has been economic rather than administrative. The Crofters

Acts of the 1880s finally gave permanent security of tenure – and heritable security – to smallholders in the Highlands and Islands. With a beast or two on the croft, some sheep on the hills, and fishing, the stubborn stayers could wrest a living from land and sea.

They never lost their pride, their sense of uniqueness, and their passion for education. The old tradition, and it was not entirely mythical, was that a 'lad o' pairts' from the croft would make his way each term to Glasgow or Aberdeen University saddled with a bag of oatmeal and a barrel of salt herring and live on them through the term with no need of money. And the tradition lasted into the 1930s.

In its own way, the hunger for self-improvement led to further emigration. Many a qualified doctor from the far north might return to practise there. Many another would seek preferment in the larger world. And the same applied to lawyers and veterinarians and teachers. World War II was not the slaughter of 1914-18, but it took many young Highlanders far away from the homelands, and many of them discovered that wider horizons were attractive.

In the late 1940s, there was an enormous migration from all over Britain to the Commonwealth countries, and it affected both Highland and Lowland Scotland. New Zealand, for instance, offered new citizens from Britain an assisted passage for a mere £10, because it was looking to expansion, and Lowlanders and Highlanders took the offer in their thousands.

A recession in 1962 had people all over the British Isles queuing to leave for Canada and America, and many of the people in line came from Scotland, both Highland and Lowland. In the province of Ontario today there is a large colony of Scots whose native accents sound

Left: A crofter family at work grinding corn, a photograph taken around 1900 by the notable Aberdeen photographer, George Washington Wilson.

even stronger than those of the people they left behind in Scotland; determined not to lose their Scottishness, they have accentuated it, and after a quarter-century of being Canadians, still sound aggressively Scots.

But subsequently, in November of 1965, the British Government had taken an imaginative step in the formation of the Highlands and Islands Development Board, a serious effort to bring the area back to life. Its first chairman, Robert Grieve, who was Professor of Geography at Glasgow University, later recalled that as a young man, he had been fascinated by the sad, romantic quality of the Highlands, and had entered photographs in competitions of ruined, roofless cottages, captioned 'Sunset on the Gael.' The work of the HIDB, in fact, was to create some kind of sunrise for the north. Its motive was to make the rest of Britain take the Highlands seriously, and to dispense with the facile romance of the sad old legend.

It pumped its available money into such

projects as resuscitating the fisheries in the Outer Isles. Britain was in the throes of entering the European Common Market, which would permit Continental fishermen to encroach on Britain's waters, and this produced complications for the Hebridean industry; but it expanded nonetheless. The Board also tried to attract heavier industries to the Highlands, and with flat land and deep water, the Moray Firth was particularly attractive. Some of the ambitious schemes went under, but in later years the North Sea oil industry would find the same Firth irresistibly attractive for its deepwater artefacts.

One of the Board's important achievements was in the apparently trivial industry of tourism, which soon took two-fifths of its budget. Subsidies made it possible for little hotels to expand their bedroom accommodation, instal central heating; on the humblest

Left: Crofters at work on Skye planting potatoes. The men are seen with the *cashrom* or foot plough, a traditional implement.

level, to provide facilities for drying wet clothes. There is a high rainfall in the Highlands. And many of the new tourists are sporting people who walk the hills and climb the mountains and join in the expanding skiing enthusiasm.

The Board has also stimulated innovative moves in Highland agriculture, side by side with the Ministry of Agriculture.

A negative effect of the enthusiastic response to the Highlands as a tourist area is the arrival of what Sorley MacLean, the Gaelic poet, has

called the White Settlers. People from the Lowlands, and even more from England, have fallen in love with the area, and bought little cottages as holiday homes. Their arrival has raised the price of small houses beyond the means of local people, and a typical result is the beautiful village of Plockton, in Wester Ross. So many of the village houses are owned, and rehabilitated, by prosperous outsiders who spend only a few summer weeks in the north, that when the holiday season is over, the village almost dies from lack of population. To

Left: The island group of St Kilda lies in the Atlantic over 100 miles west of the Outer Hebrides. In an event symbolic of the depopulation of the Highlands as a whole the population was evacuated in 1930 at their own request. The islands are now a nature reserve and the photograph shows (with modern additions) the former village on Hirta, the largest island of the group.

Left and right: Contemporary newspaper illustrations of aspects of the demonstrations in the 1880s in the Glendale district of Skye which eventually helped bring about the first Crofting Acts.

many of the newcomers, the attraction of the Highlands is the scenery, and often the weather, for there can be beautiful sunny summers in the far north. They make little contact with the local people or the local culture, and are the poorer for it. Their affection for the country can be a form of blight.

But despite that, tourism has given new life to the Highlands, along with small and large scale industrial developments. For the first

time in centuries, the population is increasing, while the population in the rest of Scotland is going down. There is new heart in the Highlands.

Another attraction to the visitor, often exaggerated, is the Highlander's patient attitude to time. There is some truth in it, and it may explain why Highlanders live long. The archetypal story is of an English visitor, lodging with a Highland farmer, who remarked that nothing

ever happened in a hurry, like deliveries or car repairs, and mentioned that the Spaniards had a word *mañana*. He wondered if the Gaels also had the same word. After a long pause, his host said, 'No, there is no word in the Gaelic with such connotations of urgency.'

It is a tale told by the Gaels against themselves. Their sense of humour has been another weapon in their survival kit; and they have needed it.

The future history of the Highlands may well be one of the great success stories of Britain.

Left: Some of the last inhabitants of St Kilda.

JAMES KEIR HARDIE was born illegitimately to a farm servant, Mary Keir, near the village of Holytown in Lanarkshire, in 1856. She later married David Hardie, and the stepfather's surname was added to the child's. At the age of ten, in hard times of unemployment, James became a baker's roundsman to help support his pregnant mother.

One morning he was late for work. He was summoned into his master's dining room, where the family was sitting round a breakfast table piled with a variety of food such as the boy had never seen, and the baker delivered this homily.

'Boy, this is the second morning you have been late, and my customers will leave me if they are kept waiting for their morning rolls. I therefore dismiss you, and, to make sure you are more careful in future, I have decided to fine you a week's wages. And now you may go.'

That night the baby was born, and in Keir Hardie's own words when he recalled the event, the sun rose on the first of January over a home in which there was neither food nor fire.

The tide of history may be diverted by such mundane events. The experience was to turn the little boy into a dogged crusader for workingmen's rights, and one whose pioneering enthusiasm would eventually drive into the minority wilderness in Scotland the Tory party which doubtless the well-fed baker loyally supported, and reduce its alternative, the Liberal Party, to a small group on the fringe of politics.

We shall return to the life of Keir Hardie. His childhood experience deserves its place at the head of this chapter because the small human drama illuminates a deep-rooted radical quality in Scotland's nature.

Even before the Industrial Revolution produced its confrontation between the new race of capitalist entrepreneurs and their employees, the seeds of trade unionism had taken root back in the eighteenth century with small, isolated groups forming self-defensive unions, friendly associations and co-operative societies. As early as 1748 there was a strike by Edinburgh journeymen tailors over wages.

Around the same time, ploughmen in Stirlingshire formed a combination to fight for improved conditions, and journeymen wool combers in Aberdeen were accused of illegal combination. The Fenwick weavers in 1769 launched the first co-operative store in Britain.

In many areas, the employers' complacent contempt for the humble needs of their workers was certainly calculated to provoke revolt. A group of Edinburgh stonemasons in 1764 published an advertisement which read: 'Over 100 years ago, when the price of vivers (food) and every other necessity of life was less than a fourth of what they presently sell at, journeymen had their wages settled at one Scots merk a day, and even that small sum was badly paid, and bilking went on. Instead of six shillings and eight pence on Saturday night, men were sometimes paid only a shilling or one and six.'

And during that century the wages, even when promptly and fully paid, had lost all real relation to the cost of living.

The employers were furious at any sign of organised rebellion, or even protest. The Woolcombers' Society of Aberdeen was taken to court by the employers who charged, 'it will prove the means of caballing, drunkenness and destroying that just and necessary subordination which ought to subsist betwixt masters and journeymen and more especially betwixt masters and their apprentices.'

When seamen struck in 1792 in Aberdeen, the city's provost asked for a warship, and for General Gordon to send troops. The authorities clearly foresaw such actions as the beginnings of red revolution. They had the example of the French Revolution before them, and the Terror in France awakened an emotional terror in Scotland's aristocrats of industry. And in a degree they were right, because the Revolution

Previous page: Sir Stanley Spencer's *Shipbuilding on the Clyde: Welders,* one of a number of his studies of Clydeside war work during World War II.

Below: George Mealmaker, pioneer radical and leader of the United Scotsmen. Mealmaker was transported to the colonies for fourteen years for sedition.

did stimulate a stampede of revolt. June 1792 brought riots in Edinburgh over the right to vote, and a dozen working people, including a woman and a boy of fourteen, were killed by cavalry at Tranent, near Edinburgh. George Mealmaker, a Dundee weaver, formed the United Scotsmen, a deliberately secret radical society, inspired by the movements across the Channel.

In the early years of the nineteenth century, little riots sprang up all over the country, some against the Highland Clearances in Sutherland which were put down by troops. In the west of Scotland, revolutionary proclamations were pinned up all over the area and there was a massive strike in 1820. In the same year the nation was startled by the Battle of Bonnymuir in Stirlingshire, in which fifty determined radicals faced up to troops. They had actually tried, and failed, to storm the Carron Ironworks at Falkirk and steal cannon for the revolutionary struggle.

At Greenock a few days later in April of 1820, the jail was stormed and prisoners were set free. Six died in the fighting, three other rebels were charged with high treason, convicted, beheaded and quartered.

It was easy for established authority to see bloody rebellion in all the protest movements. In fact, and as is common in all radical upsurges, there was a very wide spectrum of policy in the complaints. At the milder end, friendly societies were simply organisations formed to help working colleagues in distress, form small funds for the purpose, and in some cases even buy a hearse for the benefit of members, and raise further funds by hiring them to non-members for a shilling or two.

And another very innocent element very common among the reformers was a passionate adherence to temperance, something which has persisted among Scottish reformers right into modern times. They agreed with employers and the churches that drink was the curse of the working classes.

It is true that trade unionism, under the Combination Acts, was illegal, and it was not until 1824 that the Acts were repealed, in a slightly nervous show of tolerance.

Another strain in the movement was Chartism, which simply believed that an ideal society would be created by giving the vote to the people, and this feeling no doubt had some influence on the passing of the Reform Bill of 1832, though the franchise it extended limited the power of voting to people with enough property to be in favour of stability. The Chartist movement, which began in the late 1830s and flourished in the 1840s before dying out at the end of the decade, was in part a response to this disappointment. It did create a new climate of progress, all the same, and the 1830s saw the appearance of trade union newspapers and the spread of co-operative stores.

Convention of Asses or Spirit of Democracy.

These were designed to provide cheaper food for their members by buying in bulk, limiting profits and returning profits to the members periodically in the form of a dividend, so that they were savings clubs as well as retailers, and in their fairly conservative way, upholders of thrift, morality and the domestic virtues.

The union demands of the time hardly seem dangerous or revolutionary now. Farm workers in the Carse of Gowrie proposed that hours of labour should be reduced to ten hours in summer and eight hours in winter. Stonemasons desired a nine-hour day all year round. But strike action created a kind of warfare, with occasional pitched battles like the one in Glasgow in 1838, in which a blackleg had been shot and killed during a strike by cotton spinners. Five spinners were sentenced to the prison hulks at Woolwich for three years each, to spend their long days in darkness and in chains.

Some parts of the system in existence make startling reading today, including the bond-

Above: An illustration from a satirical pamphlet published in Edinburgh in 1792 attacking the radical Society of Friends of the People formed that year.

ager system, by which a male farm worker had to provide his boss with the services of a female worker for a stated number of days in each year. This strange clause survived into the early years of the twentieth century. So did the feeing system, in which farm workers and employees visited an annual feeing fair at which the workers virtually put themselves up for auction to the highest bidder, and as late as 1915 that price could be £25 and all found for a single man for six months' labour.

In the meantime the radical movement was looking to Parliament. Throughout the nineteenth century there was a political tradition by which some Liberal members of Parliament tried to speak for the interests of the workers and the unions, but in 1885 Dr Gavin Strang was elected as Crofters' Member for Caithness, and in 1888 he became a founder member of the Scottish Labour Party along with Keir Hardie, who himself failed in that year to be elected as an Independent Labour candidate.

We may digress here to look at one of those Liberals who fought for the under-dog, and he has a significant connection with Keir Hardie. A connection, but no resemblance. Robert Bontine Cunninghame Graham was a Scottish

aristocrat, an adventurer and explorer, a swordsman, a man who could out-ride the gauchos on the cattle ranch he had formerly operated in Argentina.

Above: Emblem of the Cotton Spinners' Union, one of the most effective unions in the early nineteenth century.

Right: Disturbances during a
Scottish rail strike in 1891.

Left: Pioneer socialist leader
James Keir Hardie, 1856-1915, by
H J Dobson. Hardie was a
founder member of the
Independent Labour Party.

Far left: R B Cunninghame
Graham, painted here by Sir John
Lavery, was one of Keir Hardie's
early supporters but
subsequently espoused Scottish
nationalism, and was the first
president of the National Party of
Scotland in 1928. This party
subsequently merged with
another group to become the
Scottish National Party.

He entered Parliament as a Liberal Member for North-West Lanarkshire in 1886, and did his best as a loner for the working-class cause, describing himself as a socialist. He joined in 1887 a working-class demonstration in Trafalgar Square, on a day to be dubbed Bloody Sunday, was beaten down in a police baton charge and spent six seeks in prison for unlawful assembly.

Keir Hardie stood for Parliament on the Labour ticket because the Liberal Association in Lanark had turned him down in favour of a wealthy lawyer from Wales. It was Cunninghame Graham who rushed to Lanark to persuade the Liberals to choose Hardie. They were deaf to his eloquence.

Hardie worked tirelessly as a miners' union organiser until he was invited to stand again, in England this time, at West Ham in 1892, and finally succeeded. He scandalised conservative

people of all parties by turning up to take his seat at Westminster sitting on top of a carriage and wearing not a top hat but a working-class cloth cap. Very much alone as a Member of the House, he did not transform Parliament, but he was the pioneer, he opened the crack that would eventually become a gaping breach.

And the movement was soon producing other notable personalities to proclaim the radical cause. In 1906 Tom Johnson founded the socialist weekly *Forward*, to be published in Glasgow for the next forty years as the favourite left-wing Scottish organ. It was biting, it was witty, it was totally irreverent towards the great and the powerful.

Johnson himself was one of the cheerful savage radicals who did well in Parliament. During the coalition government of World War II he was appointed Secretary of State for Scotland, and was one of the most significant people ever to hold that office, very largely responsible for launching the hydro-electric schemes which changed the Scottish Highlands radically in their own way.

The wide variations of approach in the radical cause are illustrated on one hand by the seizure in 1907 in Edinburgh of a collection of guns and ammunition which the Social Democratic Federation hoped to smuggle to Russia to serve the revolutionary cause there; and on the other by the strain of all-out pacifism which inspired sections of the movement.

By the start of World War I there was a deep schism in the ranks. There was the Labour Party, and there was the Independent Labour Party, which was particularly strong in the West of Scotland. The first group was in favour of joining in the war effort against Germany; the ILP was totally committed to pacifism. It was responsible for a mass rally in Glasgow Green in 1916 against conscription. It had already been active in the Glasgow rent strike in October of 1915, in which George Square, in the city centre, was completely packed with angry tenants, and there were armed troops lined up in adjacent side streets waiting for the order to charge. Fortunately, it never came, and the demonstration did persuade the government to bring in the first Rent Restriction Act.

Glasgow was the natural setting for acts of protest. It was not only the biggest city in Scotland, but as a great industrial centre it was inevitably a great producer of discontented workers as well as ships and locomotives. Originally built on fourteen hills, where Rome could boast only seven, it had changed from a

pleasant episcopal centre and fishing village into a dense congestion of tenements, many of them mean and unhealthy and all coated with the dark grime of air pollution.

This is not to say that everybody in Glasgow was a determined radical. The city has a self-image of a classless community, but both class and political divisions were wide, with a powerful Conservative representation in Parliament, working-class areas and pleasant bourgeois purlieus where the middle classes favoured patriotism and hanging the Kaiser. And practised the middle-class virtues of individual self-improvement, a civilised form of speech and a regard for traditional virtues.

Of course, the working class people of the city were no more totally united in anti-Government feeling than were the populations of Edinburgh, Aberdeen, or Britain as a whole. Such unanimity is very improbable in any issue. The Scottish common men volunteered in huge numbers, and were later conscripted in huge numbers, for the war in Europe, and they were slaughtered in huge numbers.

One side-effect of the war, in Scotland and England too, was a shift in the attitude to the sexes. Women had always worked for a living, usually in genteel and underpaid situations like those of shop assistants or in sweated labour situations like the jute mills of Dundee. In wartime they suddenly had to take the place of men in traditional male jobs, as tram drivers and conductors. The transport systems did not collapse. The women were quickly phased out when enough men returned from war to take their places. But women could never again be dismissed as fit only for 'women's' jobs.

Nevertheless, Glasgow was a tough and subversive city during the Great War. The Glasgow area acquired the nickname of Red Clydeside, and many of its characters took this as a compliment. John MacLean, a strange and obsessional prophet of the socialist future, almost deliberately courted martyrdom, and got it, with a three-year sentence of penal servitude for sedition in 1916 and another five years in 1918. He had the other distinction of being appointed Soviet Russia's consul in Glasgow in November 1917.

The great Soviet experiment, as left-wing and even mildly liberal Scots were to call it for decades more, was the inspiration of the times, and no criticism of it could be entertained by fervent Scottish socialists.

James Maxton was another contrast. Raised in a pleasant prosperous home near Glasgow, he attended Glasgow University, where his natural humanity pushed his ideas leftward and made him later one of the most conspicuous, and best-loved, of demagogues. Unlike John MacLean, he had an irrepressible sense of humour and of the ridiculous. He also had a wartime sentence, a year in prison. He spent much of his time in Saughton prison in Edin-

Right: A postcard picture of Anna Munro, organiser of the Women's Freedom League in Scotland in 1908. Although some socialist leaders like Keir Hardie backed the campaign for female suffrage it was not widely supported in Scotland.

Right: A demonstration in St Enoch Square, Glasgow in 1915, part of the famous and successful rent strike of that year when families, including soldiers' families, on fixed low incomes protested against landlords' raising rents to take advantage of the higher wages being paid to some war workers.

Below: The trial of the 'Red Clydesiders' in 1919. From left, Emmanuel Shinwell (later Lord Shinwell), George Ebury, David Brennan, David Kirkwood, Harry Hopkins, James Murray.

burgh trying to convert the prison officers to socialism and pacifism. It was Maxton who said that by 1916, patriotism had gone out of fashion in Glasgow.

The effect of the first war, the hideous extinction of a generation of young men in the stale-mate strategy of trench warfare, was the development of an angry cynicism that improved the fortunes of the radical cause. Relatively, at least. In the election of 1918, the country returned a solid majority of Conservatives and many Liberals. The number of

YOUR KING & COUNTRY NEED YOU

A WEE "SCRAP O' PAPER" IS BRITAIN'S BOND.

TO MAINTAIN THE HONOUR AND GLORY OF THE BRITISH EMPIRE

MORE CAMERA GLIMPSES OF THE GREAT COAST BATTLE

"THE LONDON SCOTTISH COVER THEMSELVES WITH GLORY" No. 13.

The Manless Homes of England, by Cicely Hamilton

Vol. 3   At La Bassée: The Black Watch Advance to the strains of "Hieland Laddie"   No. 65

Above and above right:
Newspaper stories from World War I featuring the exploits of Scottish soldiers. The London Scottish battalion featured above was one of the volunteer units raised by Lord Kitchener's appeal. Such 'Scottish' units were raised in several English areas from Scots resident there.

Left: A recruiting poster from World War I.

Labour MPs rose from three to seven. The increase was matched in England, and would have been greater with a different electoral system. Labour took twenty per cent of the votes, but only nine per cent of the seats.

The 'land fit for heroes to live in' promised by the Welsh Wizard, David Lloyd George, was soon a land of disillusionment. The expected economic boom ran into the ground after a year.

Workers on the Clyde called for a shorter working week, as short as thirty hours, to reduce the unemployment that was looming. Early in 1919 there was a forty-hour strike and angry crowds of strikers raised the red flag at Glasgow City Chambers. By the end of January that year, there was an occupation by troops of the city centre, and several socialist leaders, like Mannie Shinwell (many years later to be Lord Shinwell), Willie Gallacher and James Murray, were jailed for fomenting disorder.

But the 1919 strike of railway workers for higher wages was actually successful. What the Scottish miners in turn demanded was a thirty per cent increase, a six-hour day, and nationalisation of the coal industry; and a Royal Commission set up to study the proposals recommended an increase and a seven-hour day.

These were passing triumphs. Very soon the coal-owners organised a three-month lockout of the miners, and when they were allowed back, their wages, like those of other workers,

were cut by a third or even a half. Unemployment was ten per cent, and it rose to thirty in the next dozen years.

Hard times helped the labour movement's cause. At the 1922 General Election, Scotland returned thirty Labour MPs, including ten in Glasgow, who were ILP members.

History, however, is not a long struggle culminating in final triumph. It is a process of triumph and failure followed inexorably by something else. The observer of left-wing politics has detected an Orwellian form of doublethink in idealists who live by the book and therefore believe in 'the continuing revolution' but who at the same time imagine that one day the Revolution will be accomplished, in instant perfection, and that from that day it will remain, stable, blissful and unchanging. Real life, real history, denies it.

It could have seemed a triumph at the time when Labour finally took over British government in 1924, under the leadership of James Ramsay MacDonald, another of the spellbinding left-wingers; like Keir Hardie, illegitimate, from the little fishing town of Lossiemouth, who had risen to the top largely through charm and oratory. He had the enthusiastic support of the Clyde MPs, but it was a minority administration and just died away

The General Strike of 1926 was seen by some enthusiasts at the time as a triumphant rally of the forces of justice. It was certainly a struggle with plenty of local drama, and bloody clashes between strikers and police, and plenty of others between strikers and blacklegs – or non-strikers – as right-wing students rallied to keep transport services going and angry workers tried to derail tramcars,

But like many of the 'great events' of history, it was fairly muddled, and it was also helpless. The Trades Union Congress vacillated and procrastinated, and finally called out the engineers and shipyard workers two days before the strike was called off. It was, in literal fact, a nine-days wonder. It split the miners, who were locked out for six months after it ended.

There was also, inevitably, an angry response by employers against the trade unions. Many establishments refused to recognise unions or to permit their workers to join one.

One such was the Outram company, publishers of the *Glasgow Herald*, which set its face against union membership and offered a take-it-or-leave it wage package to its print workers. It was accepted. Most other Scottish workers would have knuckled under too. The wages ranged from £5.5/- (£5.25) to £7.10/- (£7.50), quite aristocratic incomes in 1926.

Two years later there was another event, this time dismissed as genuinely trivial by the labour movement. Robert Bontine Cunning-hame Graham, Don Roberto, ex-Liberal MP, nominally socialist, was elected first president of the National Party of Scotland. An irrelevance to 'serious' politicians, it nevertheless touched a chord, serious or sentimental, in great numbers of Scots. Ever since the Union of Parliaments in 1707, there were Scots who had regarded it as a treacherous surrender, and over the centuries such Scots have declared that both power and wealth tended to concentrate in the South of England; that when times were prosperous, the prosperity took a long time to drift north; but that on the other hand, when London caught a cold, Scotland instantly got pneumonia.

The Scotnats, as they were known, were a feeble political force, however. Supporters of other parties complained that they had no real policies, industrial or political or economic, except the establishment of an independent Scottish Parliament, which would then have to get rid of the Nationalists themselves and look for elections on the old party lines.

The Party therefore moved along as an enthusiastic little band of Scottish patriots, or perhaps sentimentalists, and produced its share of individualists. One such was Douglas Young, author and academic, who refused to undertake military service in World War II on the grounds that the Treaty of Union specifically left Scottish citizens out of any foreign wars being waged by England. The court took a less finicky view in interpreting the law, possibly because an acquittal would amount to a vindication and might have inspired thousands of suddenly legalistic Scots to claim the same exemption. Young accepted imprisonment gracefully and never changed his view.

We shall return to this interesting, stubborn, very Scottish phenomenon. In the meantime, the country was sharing the very hard times of all the Western world after the Wall Street crash of 1929, the year when James Ramsay Mac-Donald became prime minister of a coalition government, with the Conservatives and the Liberals, and was briskly dismissed by Labour enthusiasts as a traitor to the working class.

Scottish political enthusiasts are exactly like political enthusiasts all over the world, in their

Left: A bus is overturned during disturbances in the course of the 1926 General Strike in Glasgow.

Above: R B Cunninghame Graham speaking at the Scottish National Party's annual Bannockburn Day demonstration in 1935.

until only 1931, when times were very hard indeed. The radical Scots had the answer to depression and unemployment, which was socialism. But in Scotland itself, in the 1931 election, the country's Labour Party was virtually wiped out, winning only seven seats, about ten per cent of the seats up for grabs. It was a decade of numb acceptance of the futility of the democratic system.

The Independent Labour Party disaffiliated from the Labour Party, demonstrating the passionate individualism of the Scots – throughout their history, the Scottish churches have continually split up, split away, formed new congregations, sometimes over the most wonderfully trivial of disagreements. Some Scottish trade unions in the same period continually fissiparated. It was a weakness of organisation, or a strength of individualism, of the Scot.

Towards the end of the Thirties, the desperate state of unemployment, running at around thirty per cent in Scotland, began to improve. Conventional history credits the work of Franklin D Roosevelt, President of the United States 1932-45, with the improvement. It now looks, in retrospect, that employment increased with the beginning of preparation for World War II.

When it arrived, it is certainly true that Scotland suddenly had full employment, either in the armed forces or in war industry; a situation that may never recur. In politics, what did happen was that the membership of the Labour Party in the country rose sharply, and so did that of the Communist Party.

The Independent Labour Party in Scotland, though with few members, remained a powerful popular force. It remained totally committed to pacifism, and hundreds of its members and supporters were conscientious objectors. They had rather more tolerant treatment than their predecessors had had in the previous war, in which imprisonment had been mandatory.

Some certainly went to prison. Some were directed to essential war work, or to non-combatant service in units like the Royal Army Medical Corps. Some were totally exempted. Jimmy Maxton, the fluent and unregenerate leader of the ILP group in the House of Commons – a group of three – was free to address the House on the infamy of the war process, and to attack the nation's war leader, Wilson Churchill.

His entertaining criticisms were obviously pinpricks when the mass of the nation was united under Churchill and the war's effects on Scotland were nowhere so hideous as those of the Great War. Under leaders like Montgomery there was no question of throwing ten thousand men into a hopeless suicide to win a few useless yards of battlefield.

What happened in Scotland, apart from its share of battle casualties and war work, and

urge to find a traitor. MacDonald was merely a politician, like other politicians, and like them, his object in life was to survive. His most appalling crime, in the eyes of the faithful, was that when he was summoned by the King to be installed as Prime Minister, he did not wear a cloth cap like James Keir Hardie, but obtained the proper frock coat and a ceremonial sword. So he had sold out to ancient upper-class tradition. It may not seem like a serious crime to modern eyes. To the Labour movement, it was compounding the treachery.

The confusion of radicalism was vividly demonstrated in that same year of 1929, when the Labour Member of Parliament for West Renfrewshire, Dr Robert Morgan, a member in MacDonald's government, joined the new, even more radical movement led by Sir Oswald Mosley, the British Union of Fascists. Mosley was also a spellbinder, who saw in the Mussolini and later the Hitler conception of Europe, a marvellous united continent of total equality of opportunity, and equality of opinion.

The Ramsay MacDonald coalition lasted

Right: Ramsay MacDonald, first Labour Prime Minister, painted by Ambrose McEvoy.

Below: Sir Stanley Spencer's *Shipbuilding on the Clyde: Riveters* (detail).

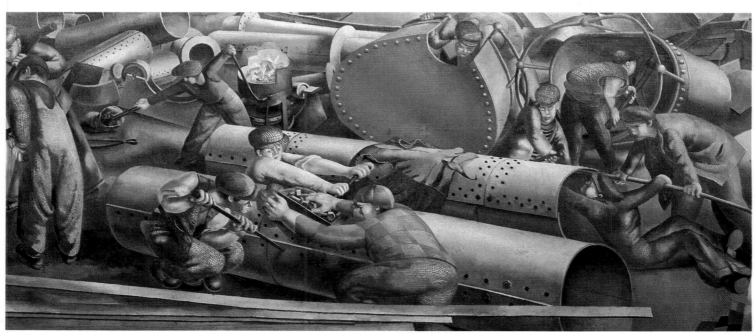

one devastating bomb attack on Clydebank, was enthusiastic planning for the postwar Scotland. The coalition government in Westminster commissioned the Beveridge Report, heralding a state in which the poorest and most underprivileged would have fair shares in the national income.

In the postwar General Election, Britain showed no gratitude for Winston Churchill's inspirational wartime leadership. He and the Conservatives were smothered in an electoral landslide, accelerated by the votes of electors still serving in the armed forces.

That postwar Labour Government, under Clement Attlee, was of course a government of the whole of Britain. But the long-standing contribution of the independent Scots was important; and important in the postwar creation of the welfare state, the kind of approach to society so long preached in little trade union halls and ILP meeting rooms.

Above: The modern face of Scottish industry, the oil terminal at Sullom Voe in the Shetlands.

Left: The Brent oil field in the North Sea. Nearest the camera is the Brent A production platform.

If remote areas like Scotland were not sharing in the general future prosperity, Government intervention could correct the error. The big motor corporations of the English Midlands were directed to open factories in Scotland, and prosperity and employment were dispersed. British Leyland opened a truck factory at Bathgate and became the main employer of the town. Early in the sixties, the Rootes motor group was encouraged to set up a Scottish branch factory at Linwood, outside Glasgow, to manufacture its new baby car, the Hillman Imp. Employment boomed.

The visionary hydro-electric schemes dreamed of by Tom Johnson became a reality, and they still serve.

The situation in the car and truck industry was another thing. The Linwood factory, and to a slightly lesser degree the Bathgate factory had very turbulent labour relations. The Rootes group itself ran into troubled financial times and was taken over by Chrysler of America, which had troubles of its own. Inevitably, the remote branch factory was first to go under. Bathgate followed.

What was not obvious on the spot was the recession that was gradually to spread over Western Europe and America. And the popular belief was still that when the South of England prospered, the prosperity took ages to travel north; but that when London sneezed, Scotland got pneumonia.

Scotland became fertile soil for another brand of radicalism – Scottish nationalism. In 1952 the National Party organised the Covenant, a national poll on the question of independent government for Scotland. In two years, two million signatures in favour were collected. The apparent enthusiasm did not translate itself into votes, however, though Winnie Ewing was elected for the SNP at a by-election in Hamilton in 1967. She later lost the seat, but SNP support in the country continued to grow until the General Election of October 1974 when the SNP won eleven seats and polled thirty per cent of the vote in Scotland.

There was still, clearly, a groundswell of feeling in favour of some kind of devolution in the country, and the Labour Government in

Below: The eleven Scottish Nationalist MPs assemble for the opening of Parliament in October 1974, the largest representation the party has yet gained.

March 1979 organised a referendum to test the national will. The arrangement itself was criticised by many nationalists. It required that at least forty per cent of the electorate should vote for devolution for the result to be valid. One couple reported that they appeared on the electoral register with two addresses, one at their front door and one at their back door, so that if they voted yes at one address, they were abstaining at the other. The majority in favour of devolution, for some kind of separate assembly in Edinburgh, was 52 per cent of those who voted, but this amounted to less than forty per cent of the total electorate and the referendum was declared void.

The Parliamentary representation of Scotland at Westminster has remained predominately Labour by a large majority since the war, in spite of contrasting swings in Britain as a whole, and there were in 1986 only two SNP members in the House.

There were also small straws in the wind which seemed to bring the SNP back into favour. In 1985, the British Steel Corporation, still nationalised as it had been by a Labour Government, decided to close the cold-rolling mill of Gartcosh, as part of a rationalisation process, and transfer its operation to plants in Wales. It was seen by Scottish politicians, and not all of them left-wing radicals, as the beginning of the run-down of Scotland's entire manufacturing industry.

In the ensuing arguments, the Scottish National Party suddenly seemed to have fresh significance. If its voice had been heard earlier, such remote decisions could hardly have been made. In a brief period in 1986, in local government by-elections, the Party took five seats from Labour.

And so, as at any time in history, the next development is a mystery. History is made not only by national leaders, rather is it grasped by leaders who have an instinct for the strange forces that shape it. The people who have made Scottish history were people who did not dictate it, but who were sensitive to the unspoken urge of ordinary people.

That is, perhaps, (and this history does not claim to know better than others) what history is about.

This is not the definitive history of Scotland. There will be no definitive history of Scotland. The country has arrived, once more, at a painful and difficult time.

What it has had is a previous experience of painful and difficult times; a capacity to survive them; and a tough, resilient, passionate, compassionate, humorous capacity to create out of them something quite unexpected. Its story is one of battered spirituality, intellectual curiosity, outside pressure and inner dissension – and survival.

The history of Scotland is about to begin. Again.

Above: Protesters demonstrating against the planned closure of the Gartcosh steelworks parade outside the larger Ravenscraig plant which many believed to be potentially the next on the list if Gartcosh closed. Despite the protests, the closure of Gartcosh went ahead at the end of 1985.

Index

Page references in *italics* refer to illustrations and captions.

Acknowledgments

The publisher would like to thank Donald Sommerville who edited this book, Martin Bristow who designed it, Wendy Sacks who did the picture research and Penny Murphy who compiled the index. We would also like to thank the following picture agencies, institutions and individuals for supplying illustrations on the pages noted:

Aberdeen Art Gallery & Museums: pages 166(bottom), 167
Aberdeen University Library: pages 85(right), 104(top), 157, 169 (GW Wilson Collection), 171(top-GW Wilson Collection)
BBC Hulton Picture Library: pages 1, 4-5, 25(top), 31(top), 32, 37(both), 45(both), 48(top), 53(bottom), 56(bottom), 61(bottom), 80(top), 85(left), 88(top), 92(bottom), 102(bottom), 116(top), 118(bottom), 124(both), 125(bottom), 128(bottom), 136(both), 146(bottom), 150, 152, 166(top), 168, 173(bottom), 176, 177
British Library: pages 19(bottom), 30, 64, 65(top)
British Petroleum; page 187(top)
Britoil: page 109
Michael Brooks: pages 6-7, 10, 11(bottom), 14, 15(bottom), 18, 19(top), 22(top right), 26-7, 42-3, 46(bottom), 55(both), 71(top), 75(top), 79(top), 91(bottom), 102(top), 103(bottom), 107(both), 114(bottom), 119(top), 127(top right), 151(top)
City Art Centre, Edinburgh (Antonia Reeve): pages 22(bottom), 33, 38, 39, 47(bottom), 50, 54(bottom), 67, 70, 82-3, 119 (bottom), 144, 146(top)
City Art Centre, Edinburgh (Tom Scott): pages 93, 121
Dundee Art Galleries & Museums: pages 22(top left), 46(top), 62-3, 73(top), 81(top left), 120(both), 126(top), 137(top), 142-3
John Frost Newspapers: page 183(both)
The Glasgow Herald: pages 137(bottom), 181(both), 184, 185, 188, 189
Glasgow Museums & Art Galleries: pages 9(both), 34(right), 58-9, 59, 66, 71(bottom), 75(bottom), 78(bottom), 94-5, 114(top right), 123(bottom), 133(bottom), 138, 140(top), 154-5, 159, 178(bottom left)
Her Majesty the Queen: pages 2-3, 34(left)

Hunterian Art Gallery, University of Glasgow: pages 40, 86(both), 87(top), 127(top left), 151(bottom)
Imperial War Museum, London: pages 174-5, 182, 186(bottom)
Mansell Collection: pages 11(top), 16, 17, 20, 24, 28, 49, 52, 53(top), 56(top), 57(top), 61(top), 65(bottom), 68(both), 69, 76(all three), 80(bottom), 96, 100, 105, 110-11, 112(bottom), 113, 116(bottom), 117, 129, 145, 147(bottom), 172, 173(top), 179
The Mitchell Library, Glasgow: pages 99(top), 101, 103(top), 122, 128(top)
National Army Museum, London: pages 47(top), 73(bottom), 161(both)
National Galleries of Scotland: pages 31(bottom), 35(top), 36(top), 41, 44(both), 48(bottom), 51(both), 54(top), 57(bottom), 60, 72, 74, 77, 79(bottom), 81(top right and bottom), 84, 87(bottom), 90, 97(bottom), 114(top left), 125(top), 126(bottom), 127(bottom left and bottom right), 132(left), 133(top), 149, 156, 160, 178(bottom right), 186(top)
National Library of Scotland: pages 88(bottom), 92(top), 112(top)
National Maritime Museum, London: page 104(bottom)
National Trust for Scotland: pages 15(top), 91(top), 134(both), 135(bottom), 139(all three), 147(top), 148(both), 171(bottom)
Peter Newark's Historical Pictures: page 13, 21, 25(bottom), 78(top), 115, 118(top)
People's Palace Museum: pages 97(top), 98, 99(bottom), 130-1, 135(top left and right), 178(top), 180
Perth Museum & Art Gallery: pages 29, 164, 165
George Philip & Son Ltd: page 23
Royal College of Surgeons, Edinburgh: page 89
The Royal Commission on Ancient Monuments, Scotland: pages 12, 36(bottom)
The Scotsman: pages 140(bottom), 141, 153
Scottish Tourist Board: pages 8, 123(top), 158(both)
Shell International Petroleum Company: page 187(bottom)
Skye Museum: page 170
Sotheby's: page 35(bottom)
Tate Gallery: pages 162-3